The Piano Compendium

A Selection of Pieces for Piano

Book 2
Grades 4-6

KONSTANTINOS PAPATHEODOROU

Erebus Society

First published in Great Britain in 2018
Erebus Society

First Edition

Arrangement © Konstantinos Papatheodorou 2018
Cover © Constantin Vaughn 2018

ISBN 978-1-912461-07-3

www.erebussociety.com

TABLE OF CONTENTS

GRADE 4

Minuet in C Minor

Franz Joseph Haydn

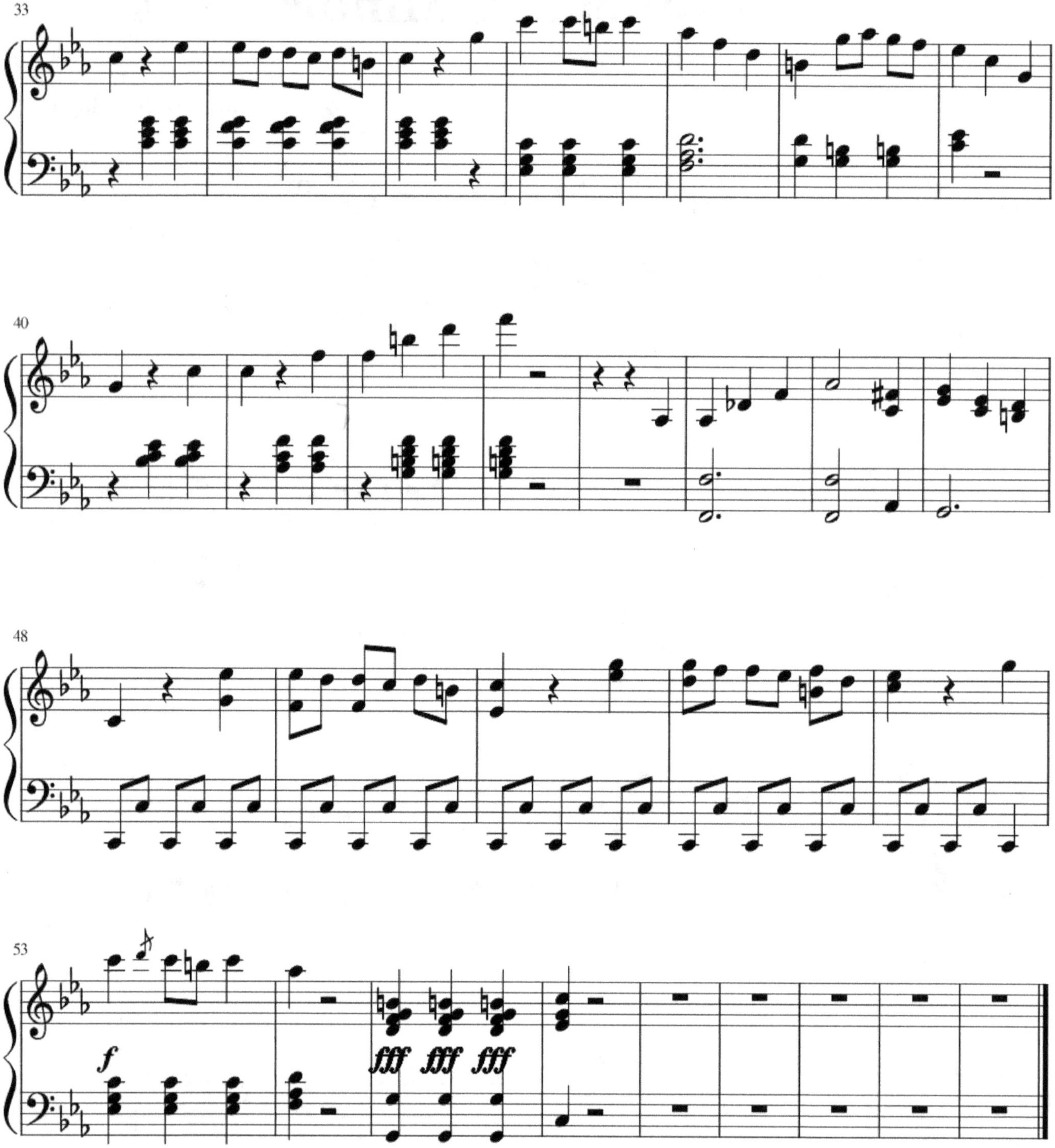
33
40
48
53
f
fff
fff
fff

Sonatina in C Major

Opus 20, No 1 – 1

Friedrich Kuhlau

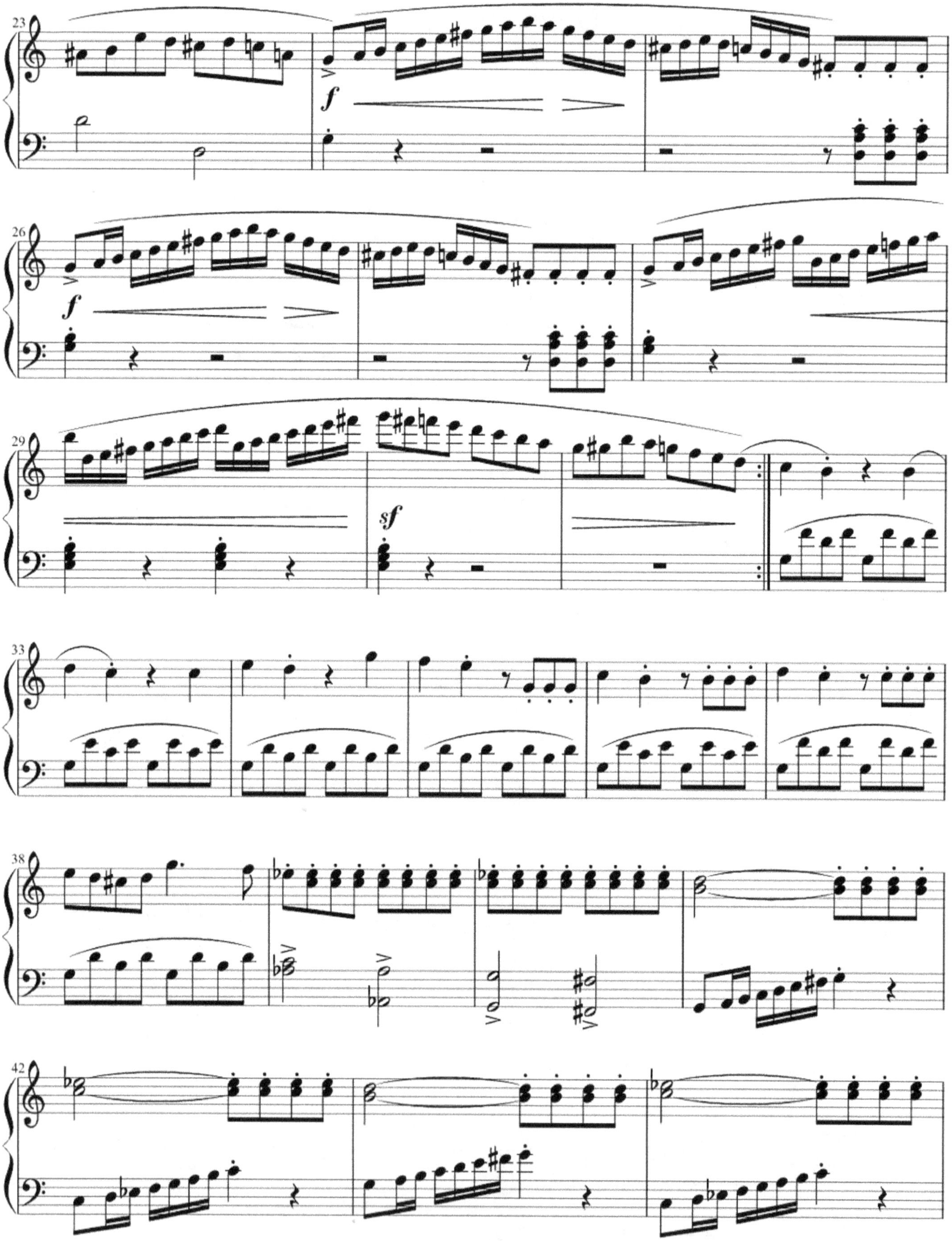
23
f
26
f
29
sf
33
38
42

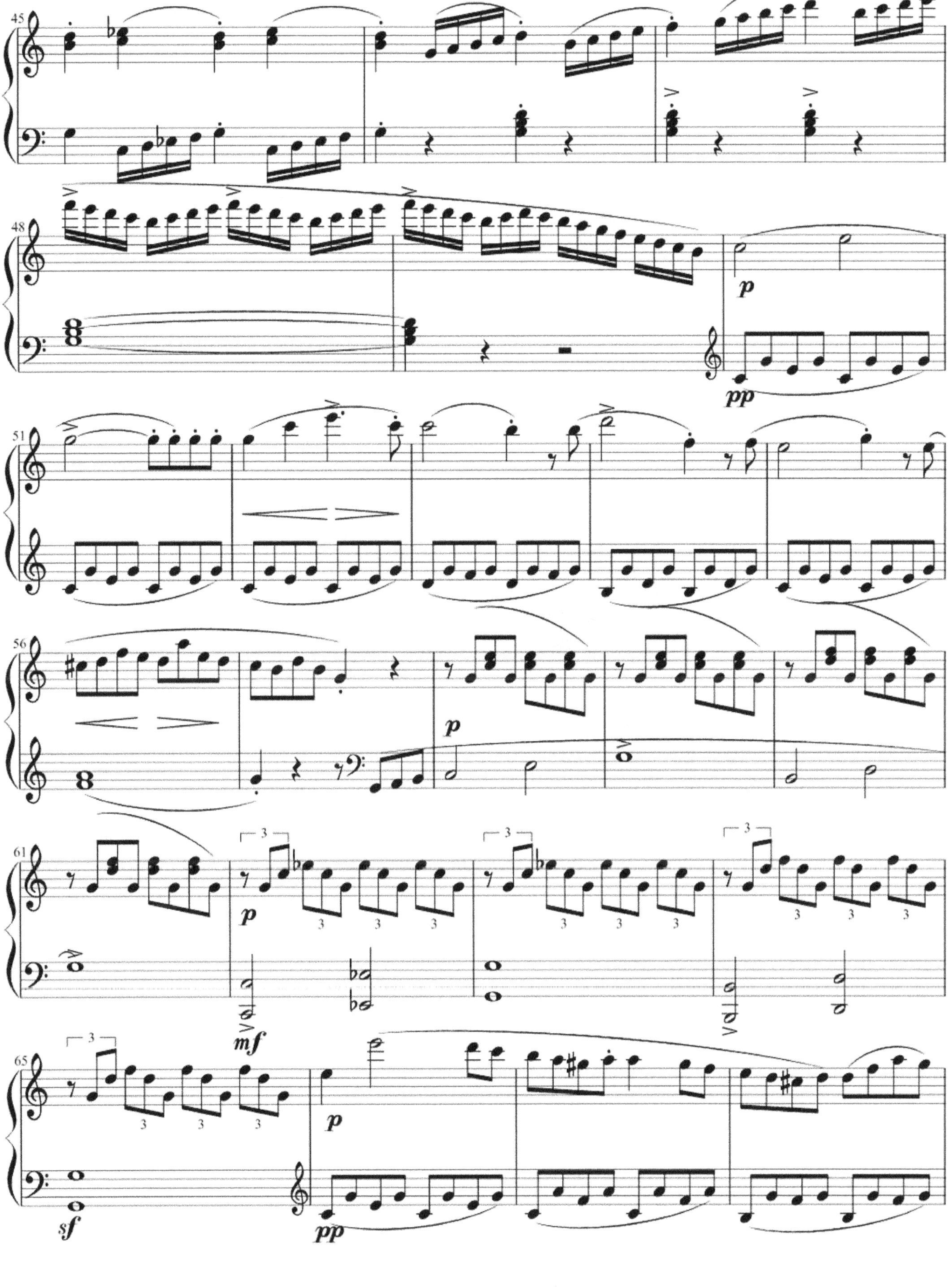

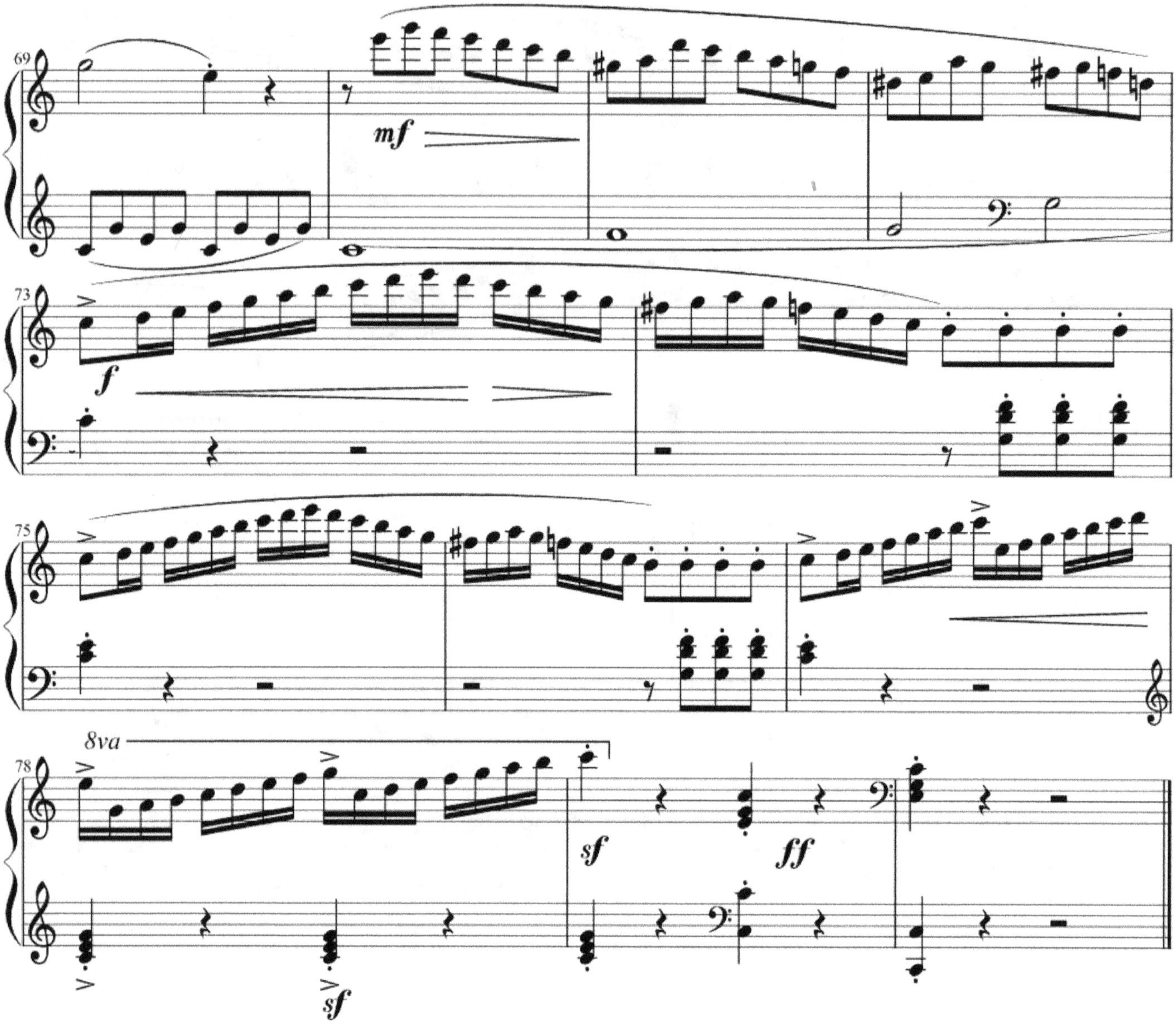
69
mf
73
f
75
8va
78
sf
ff
sf

Sonatina
Opus 20, No 1

Friedrich Kuhlau

Schelm

Heinrich Hofmann

Waldvöglein

Heinrich Hofmann

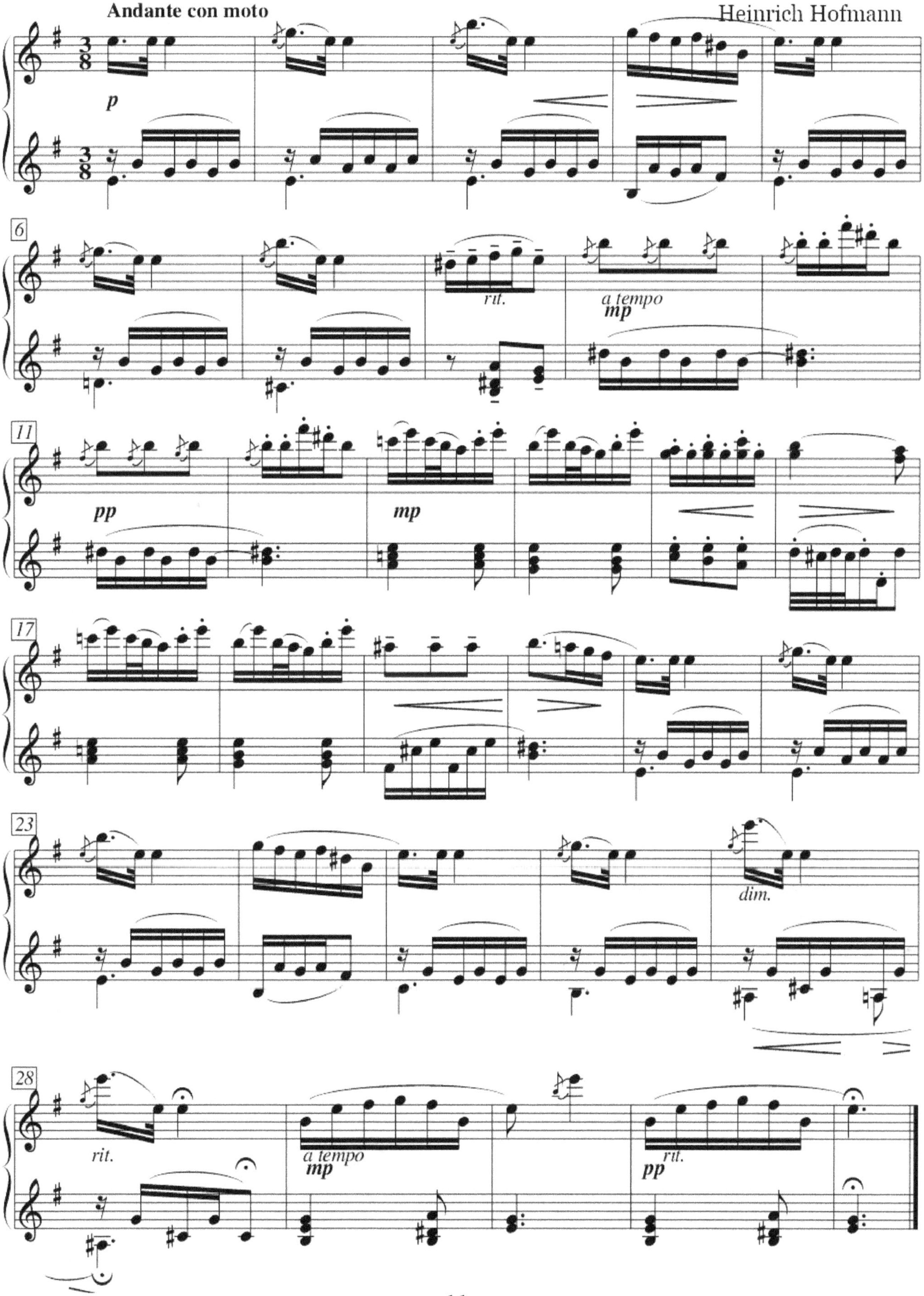

Sonatina 1

Johan Baptist Vanhal

13

Invention No 1

Johann Sebastian Bach

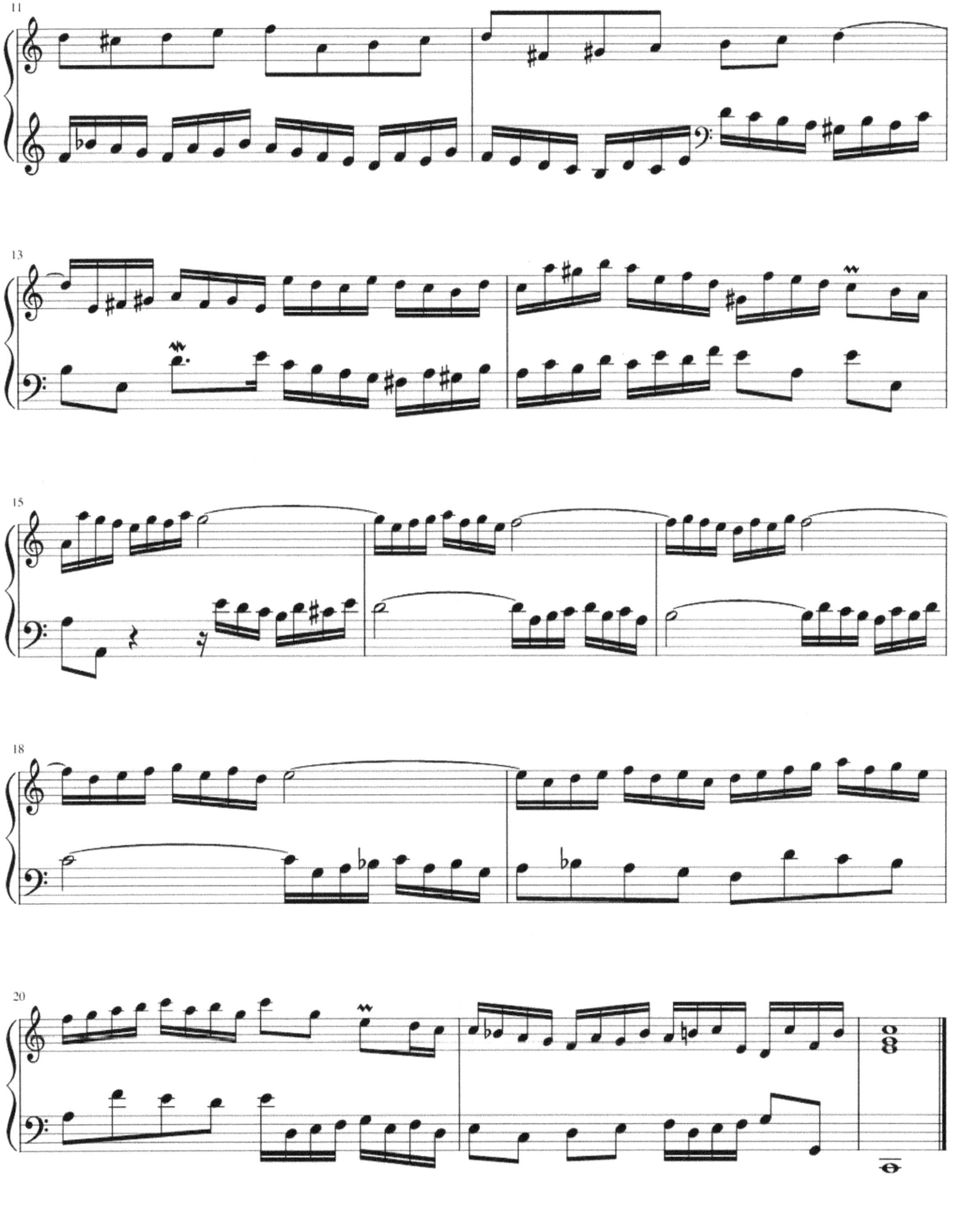
11
13
15
18
20

Bagatelle No 25 in A Minor
Für Elise

Ludwig Van Beethoven

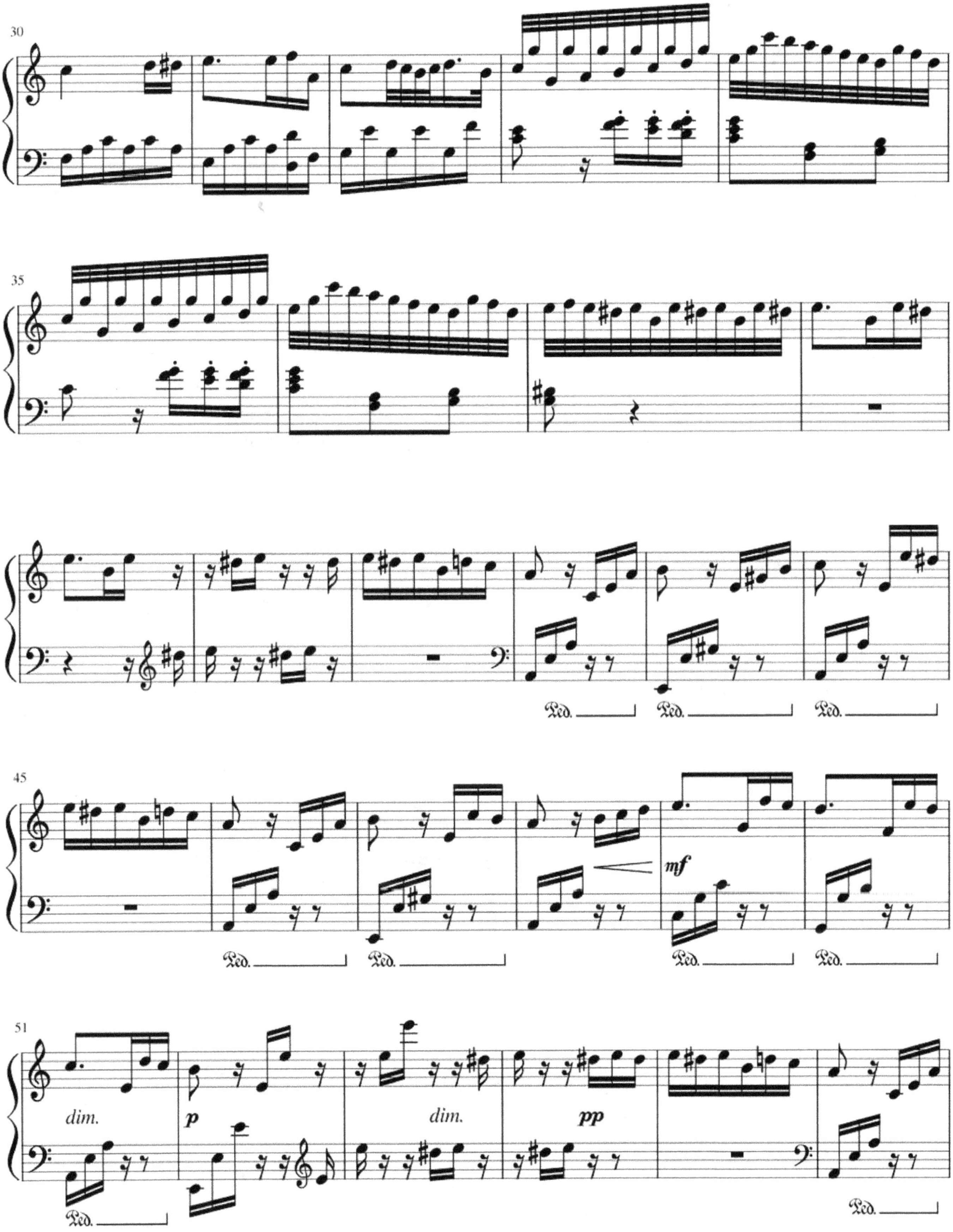
30
35
45
Ped.
mf
51
dim.
p
pp

57
Ped.
cresc.
f
63
dim.
p
cresc.
68
(cresc.)
f
dim.
p
76
pp
cresc.
dim.
80
(dim.)
pp
Ped.
Ped.
Ped.

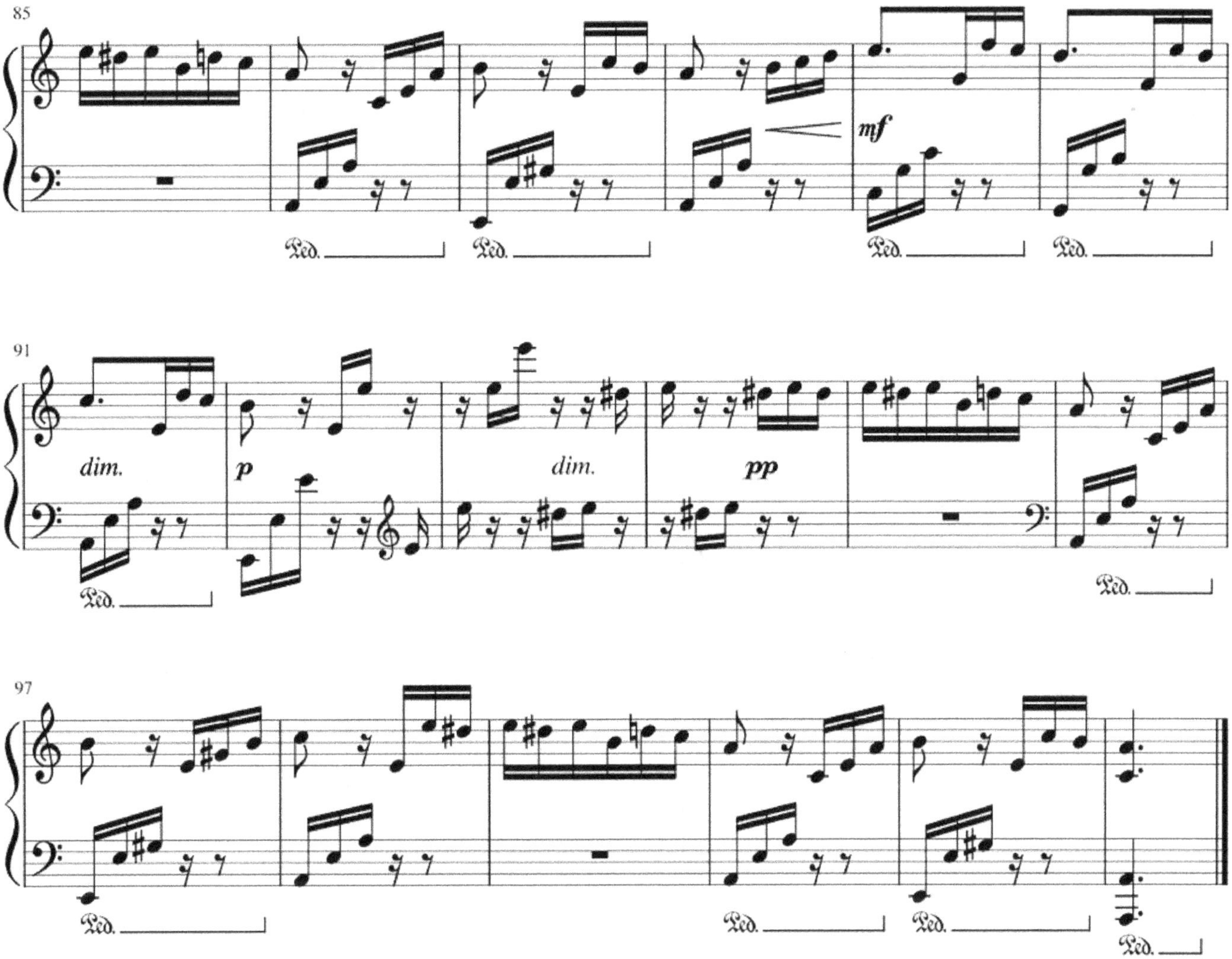
85
mf
Ped.
91
dim.
p
dim.
pp
Ped.
97
Ped.

Opus 36, No 1
First Movement

Allegro

Muzio Clementi

Opus 56, No 2

Robert Schumann

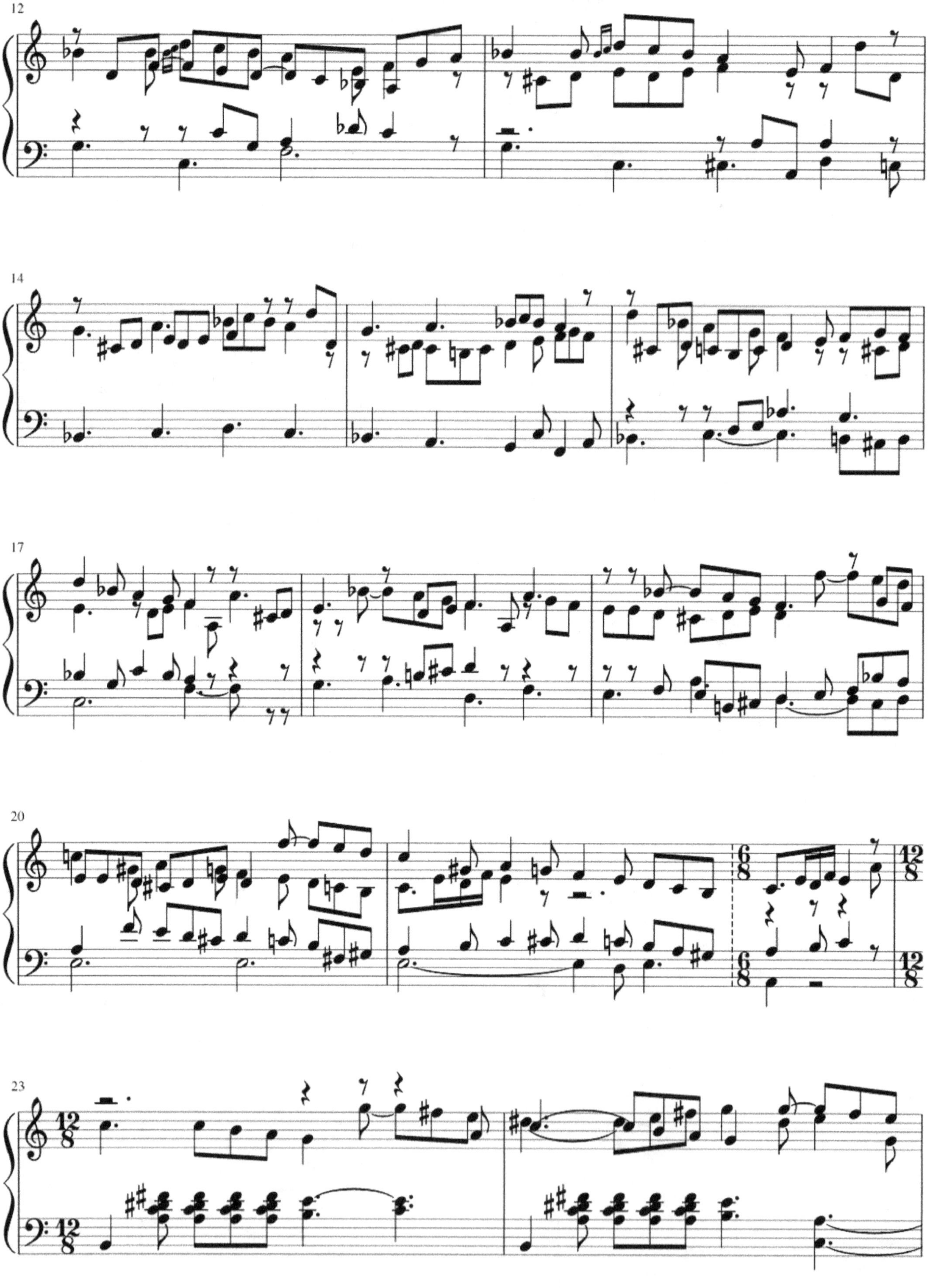
12
14
17
20
23

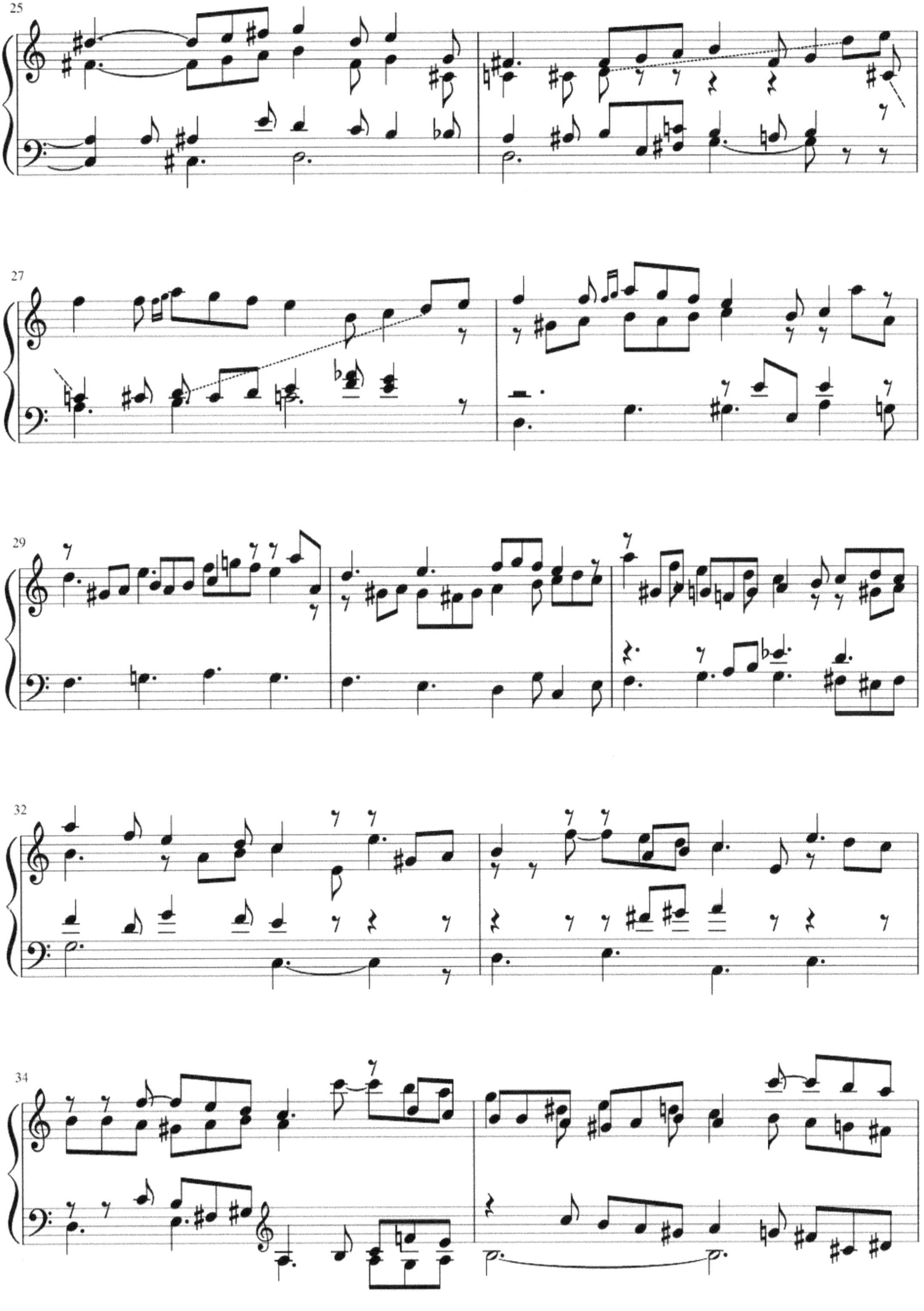
25
27
29
32
34

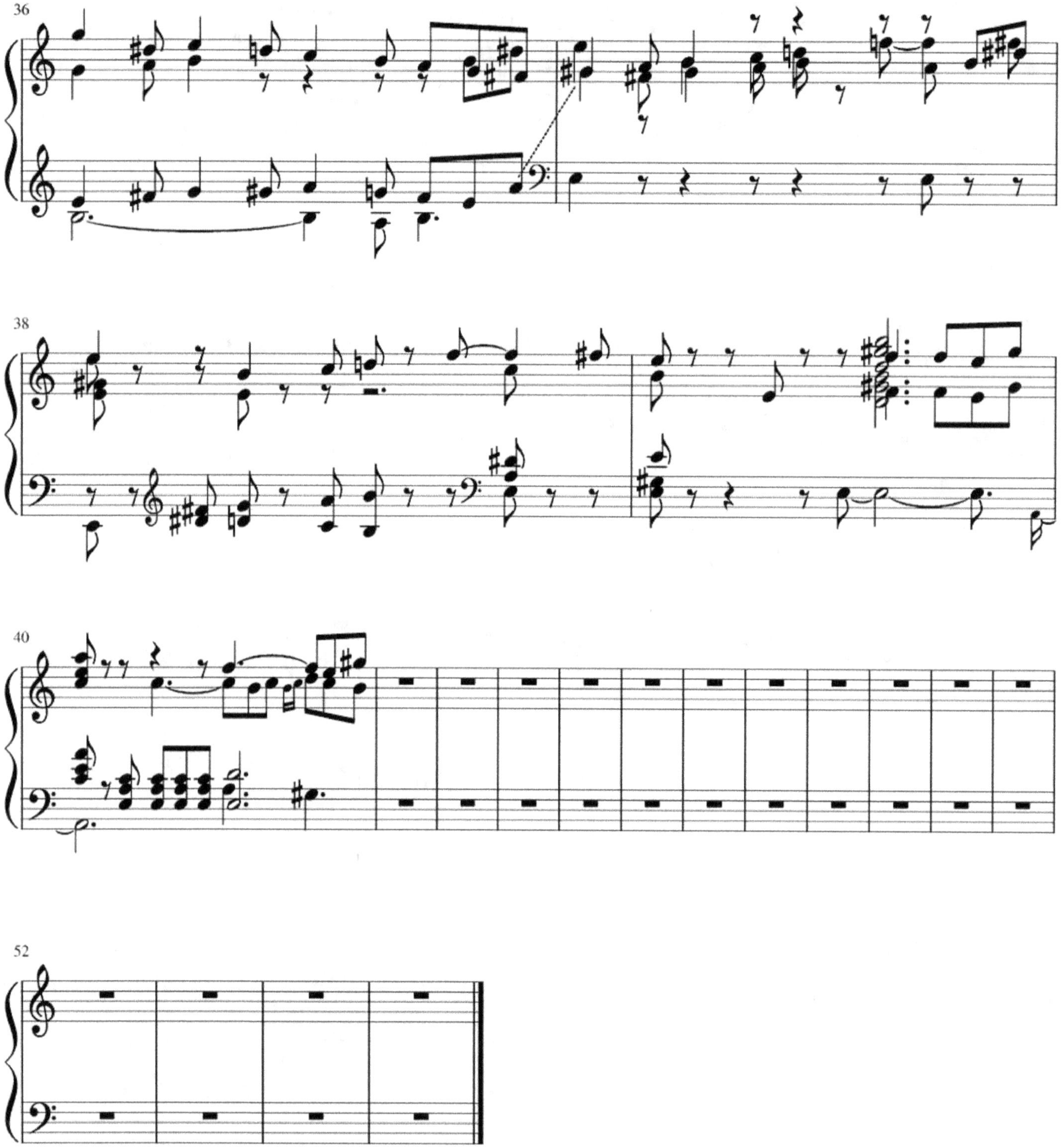
36
38
40
52

The Merry Farmer
Opus 68, No 10

Robert Schumann

Allegro animato ♩ = 120

GRADE 5

Polonaise in G Minor

Carl Philipp Emanuel Bach

Sonata in E Major

Domenico Scarlatti

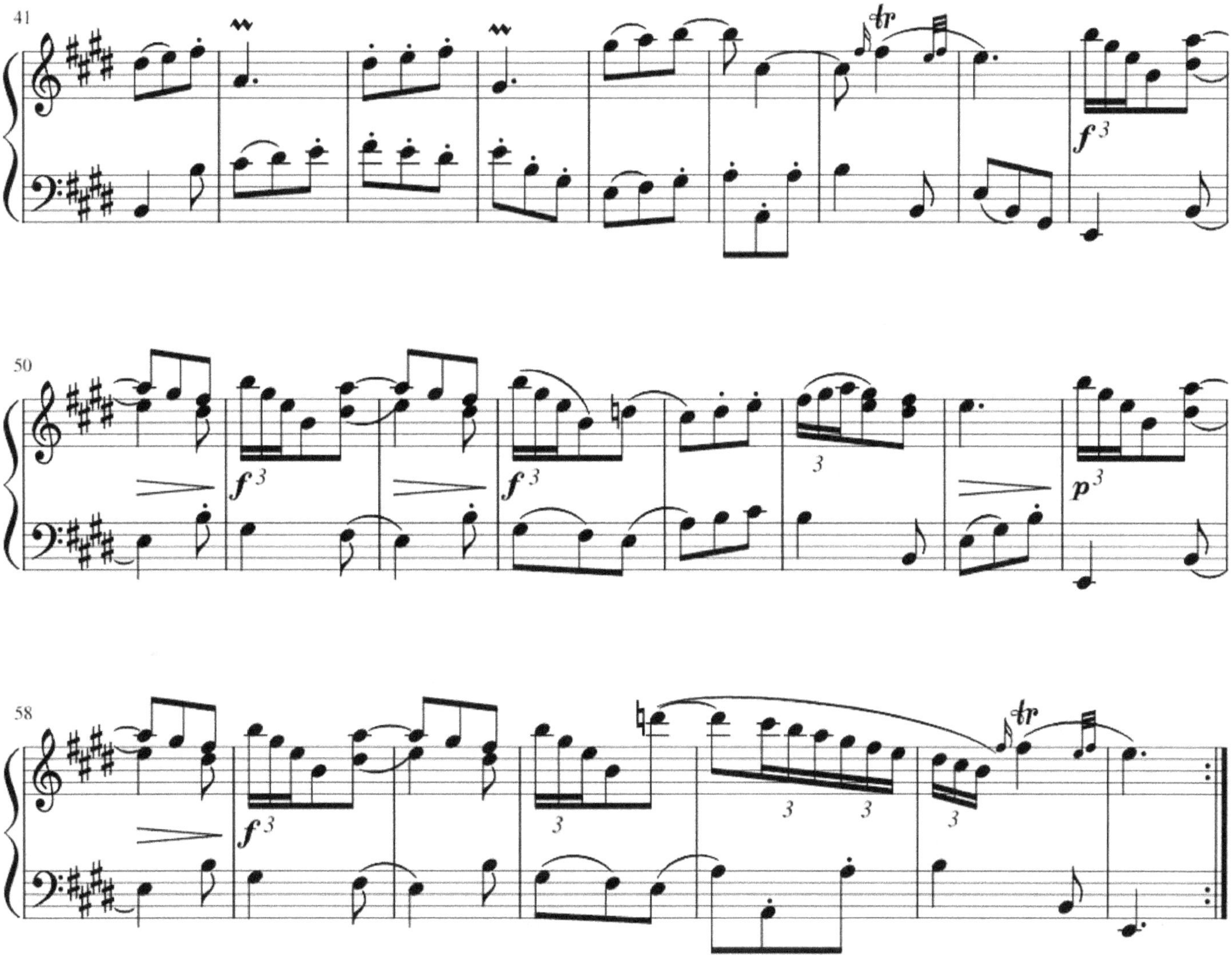
41
50
58

Sostenuto in E♭

Frédéric François Chopin

Suite No 1 in G Major

Henry Purcell

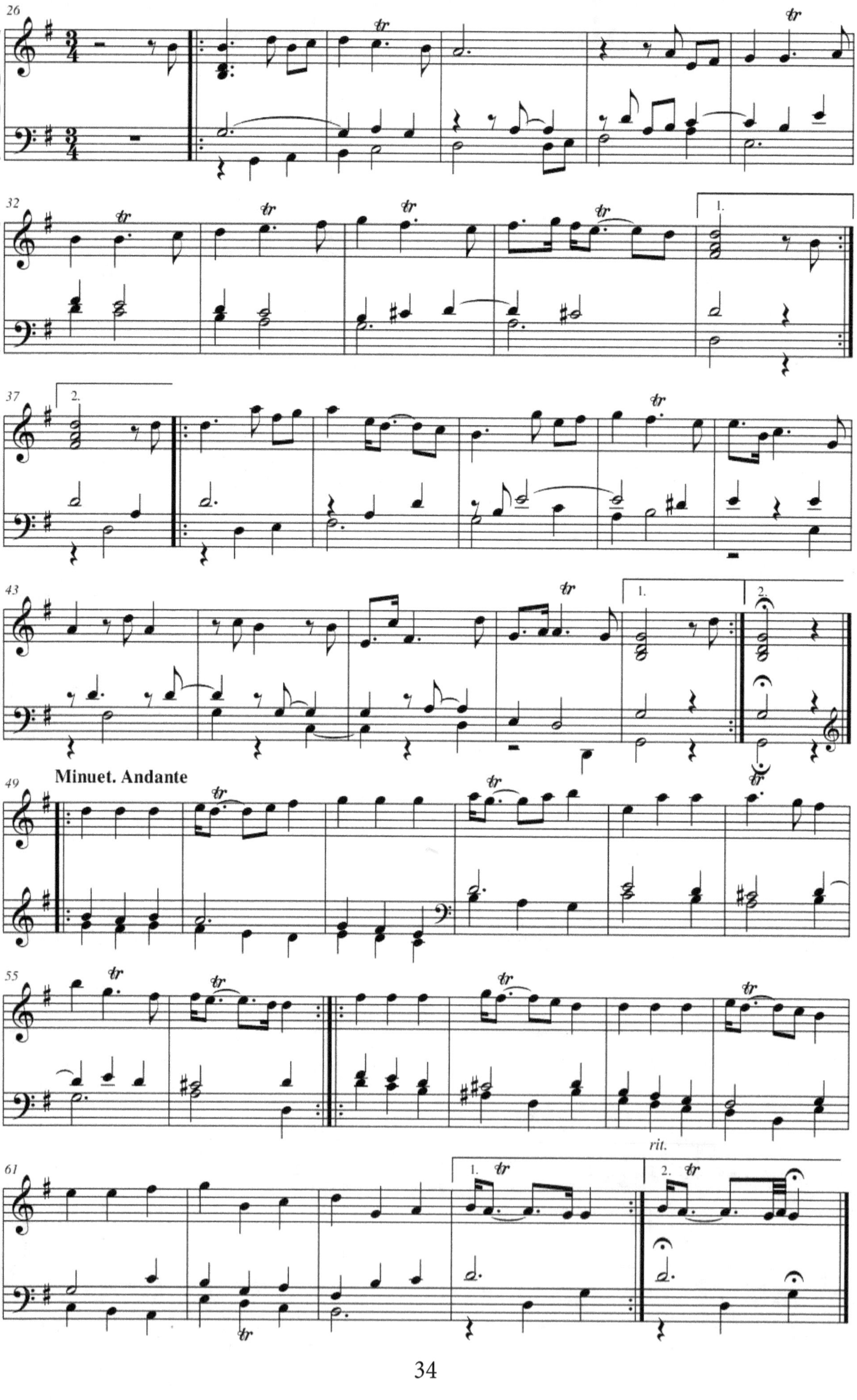
Minuet. Andante
rit.

This the Ever Grateful Spring

Henry Purcell

Thus the ev - er grate - ful Spring,

thus the ev-er-grate - ful Spring Does her year-ly tri - bute bring, does her year-ly tri -

- - - bute bring, does her year-ly tri - bute

bring, does her year-ly tri - bute bring; All your

sweets be – fore him lay all your sweets be – fore him lay, Then round his

al – tar sing and play, All, all all, all, all, all, all your

sweets be fore him lay, Then round his al – tar sing and play, then round

his al – tar sing and

play. Thus the ev - er grate - ful Spring Does her year - ly tri – bute

bring, does her year - ly tri – – – bute

bring, does her year - ly tri – bute bring, does her year - ly tri –

– – – bute bring.

Prelude in E Minor
BWV 938

Johann Sebastian Bach

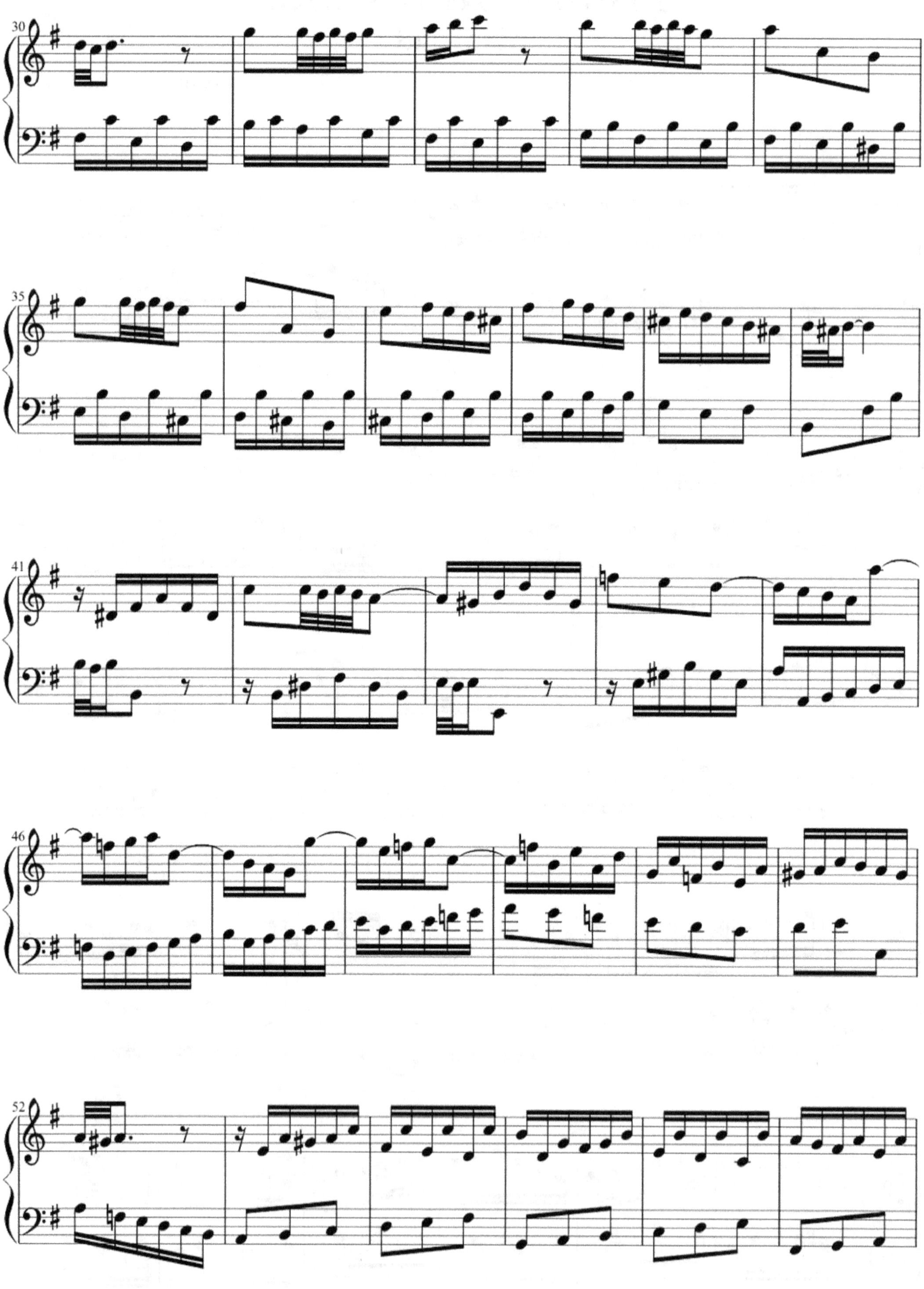
30
35
41
46
52

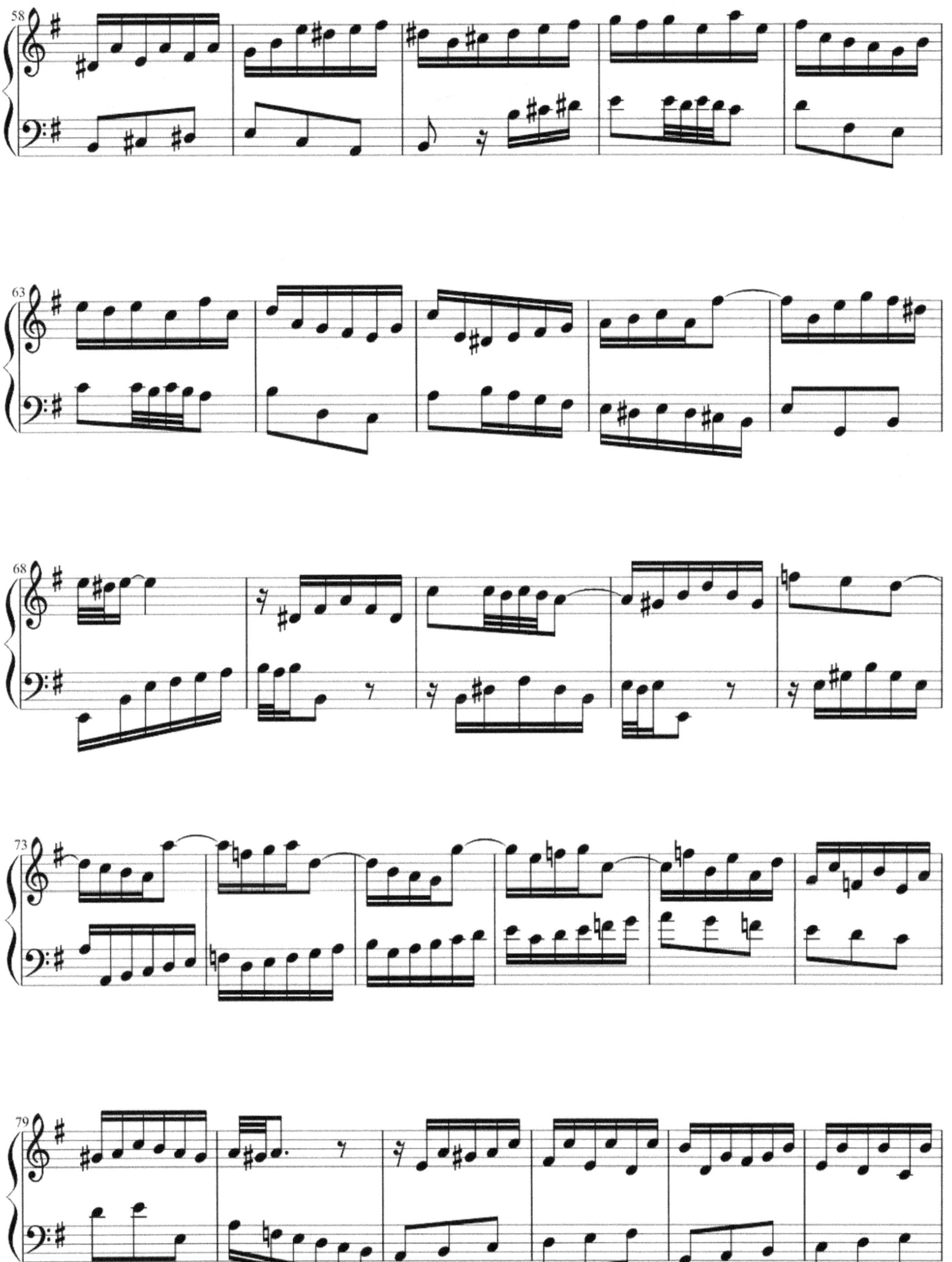
58
63
68
73
79

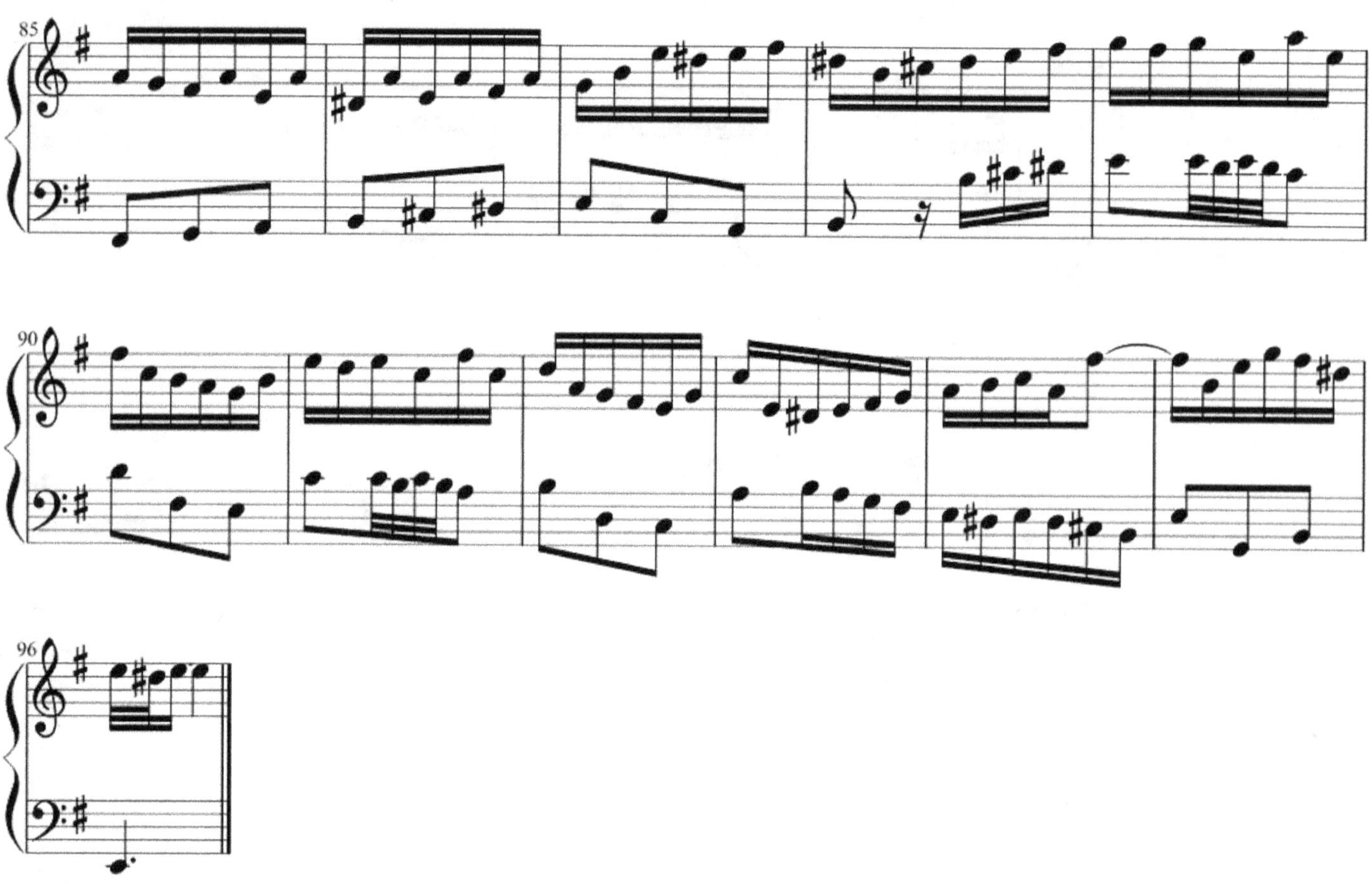
85
90
96

Invention No 4 in D Minor
BWV 775

Johann Sebastian Bach

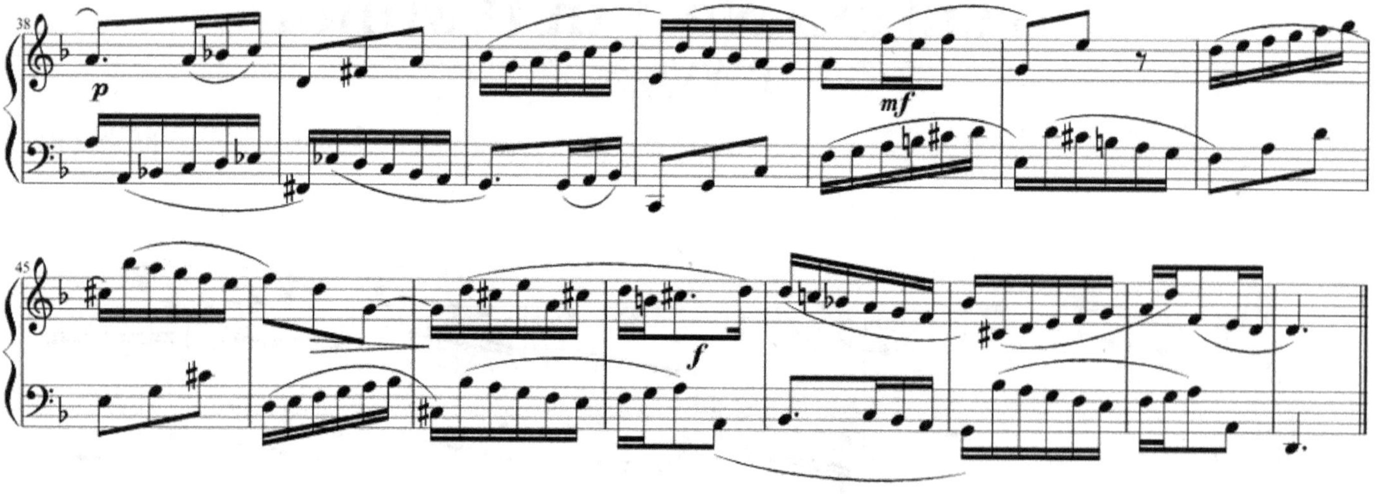
38
p
mf
45
f

Prelude and Fugue in G Major

Johann Sebastian Bach

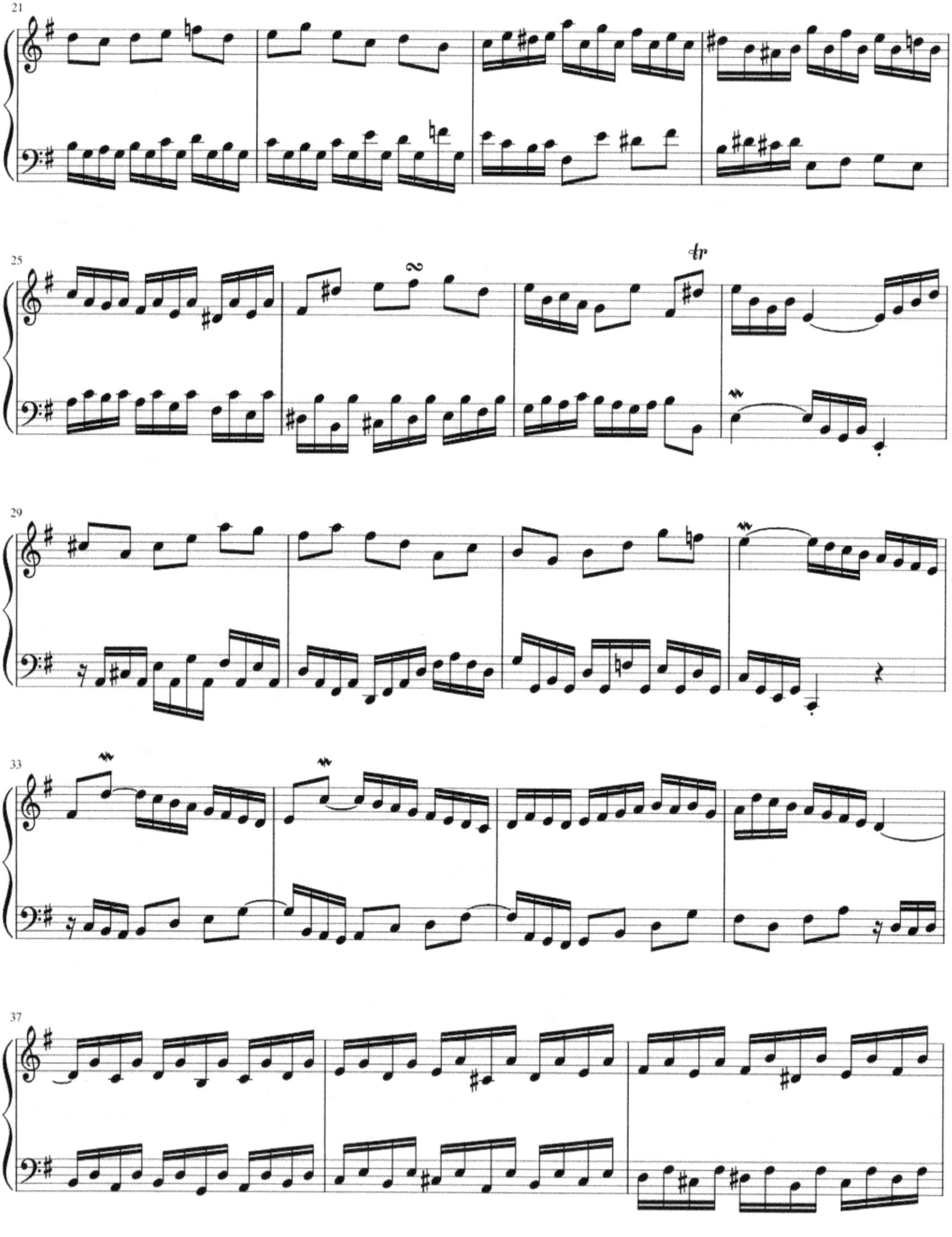
21
25
29
33
37

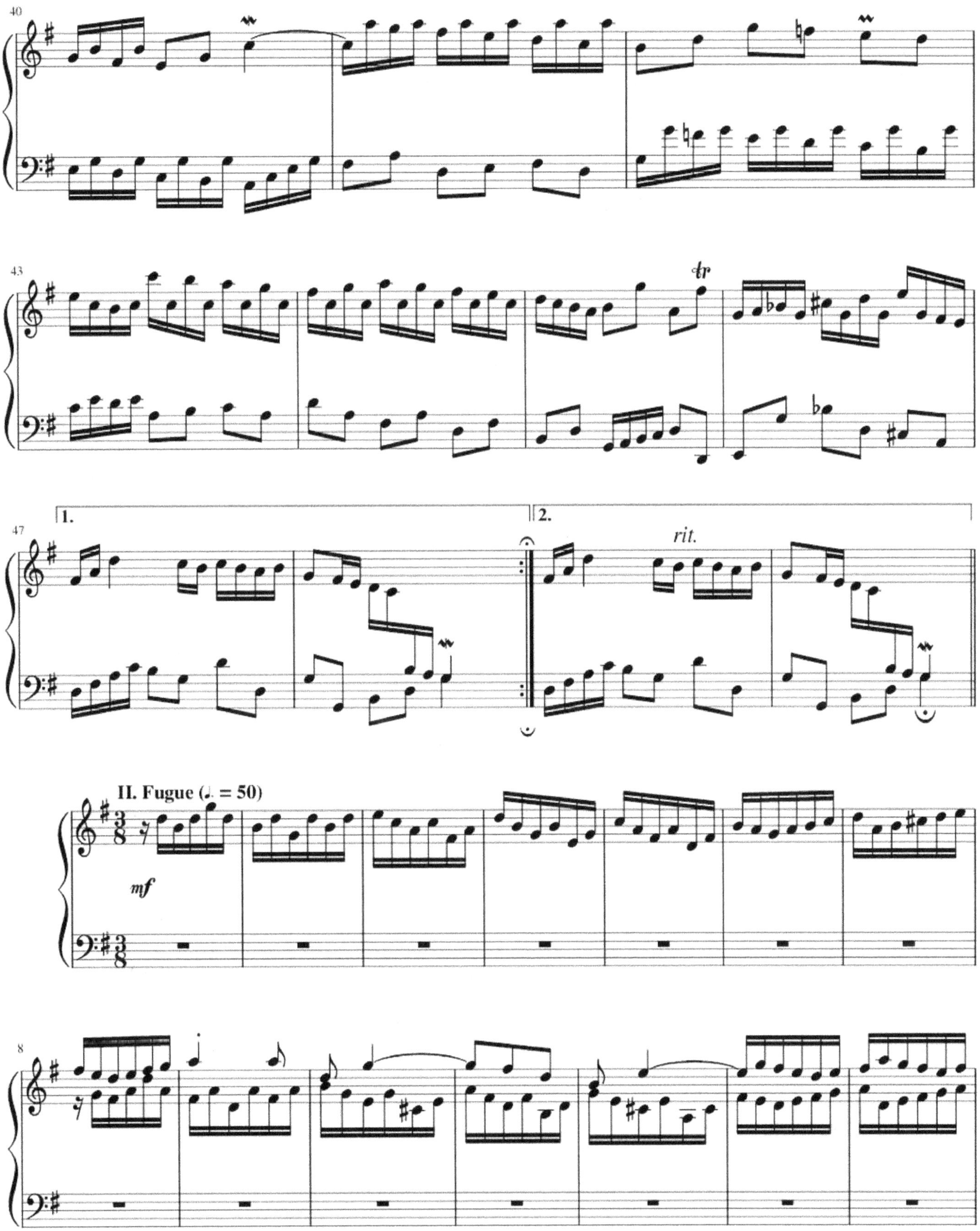
tr
1.
2.
rit.
II. Fugue (♩. = 50)
mf

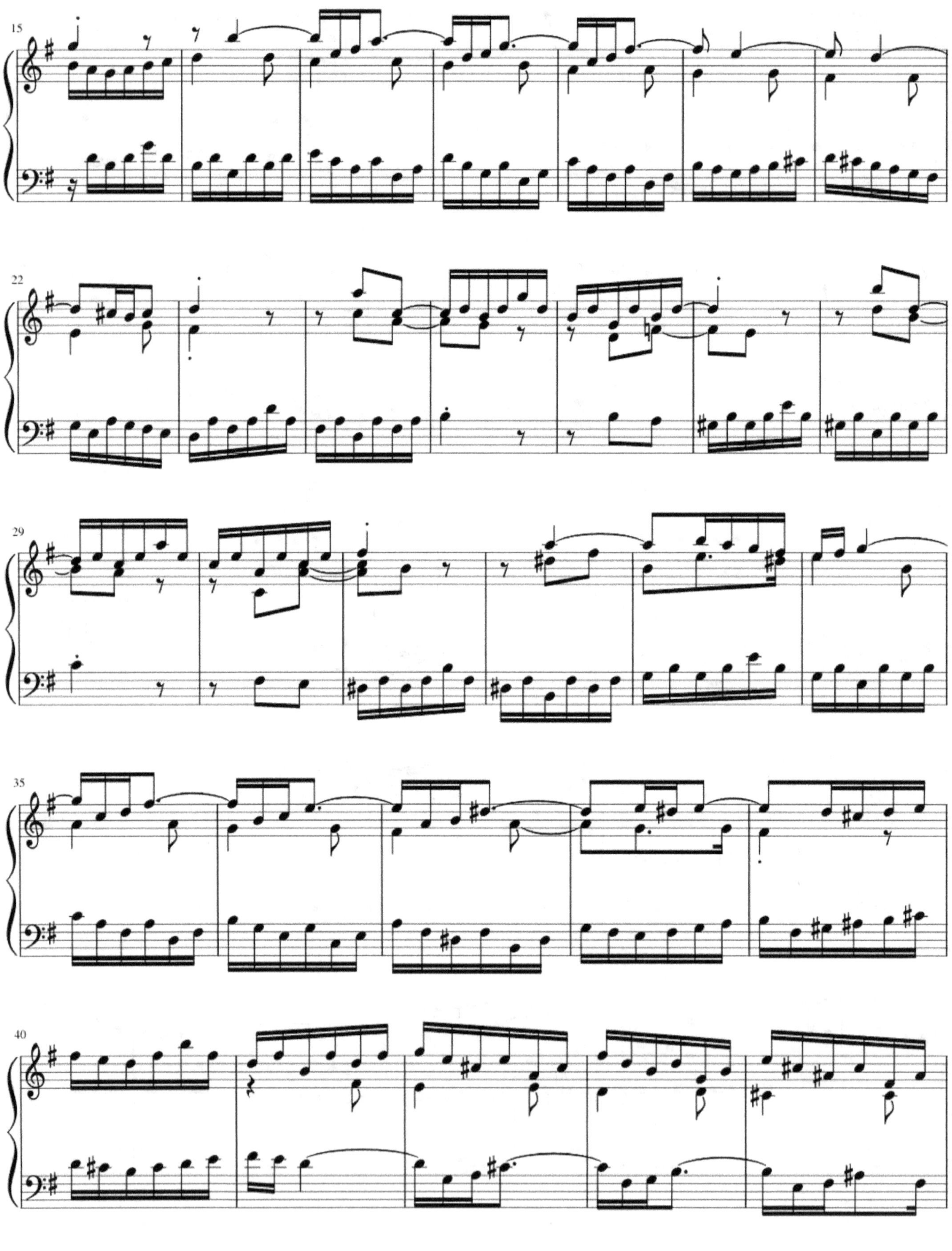
15
22
29
35
40

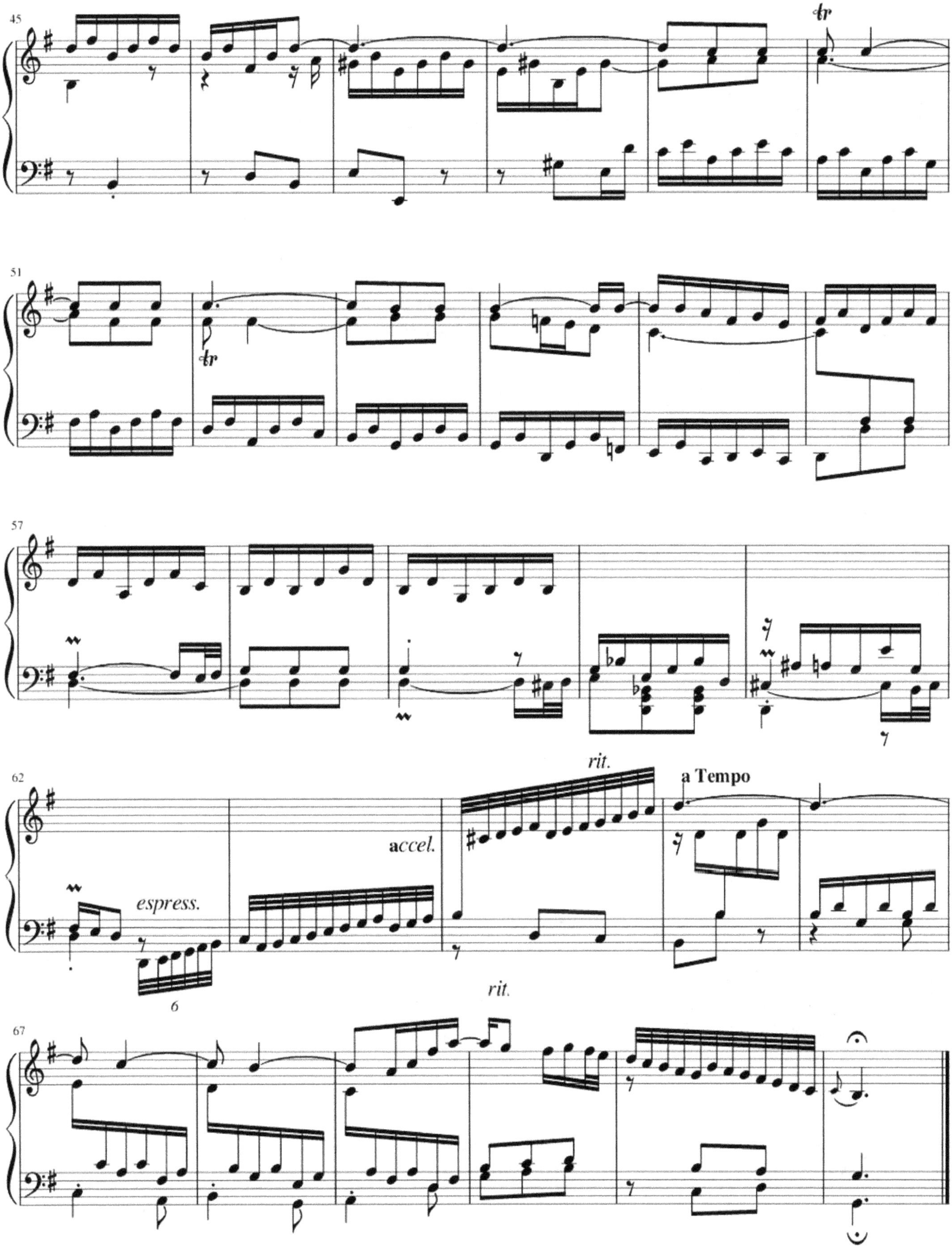
45
tr
51
tr
57
62
rit.
a Tempo
accel.
espress.
6
rit.
67

Opus 49, No 2

Ludwig Van Beethoven

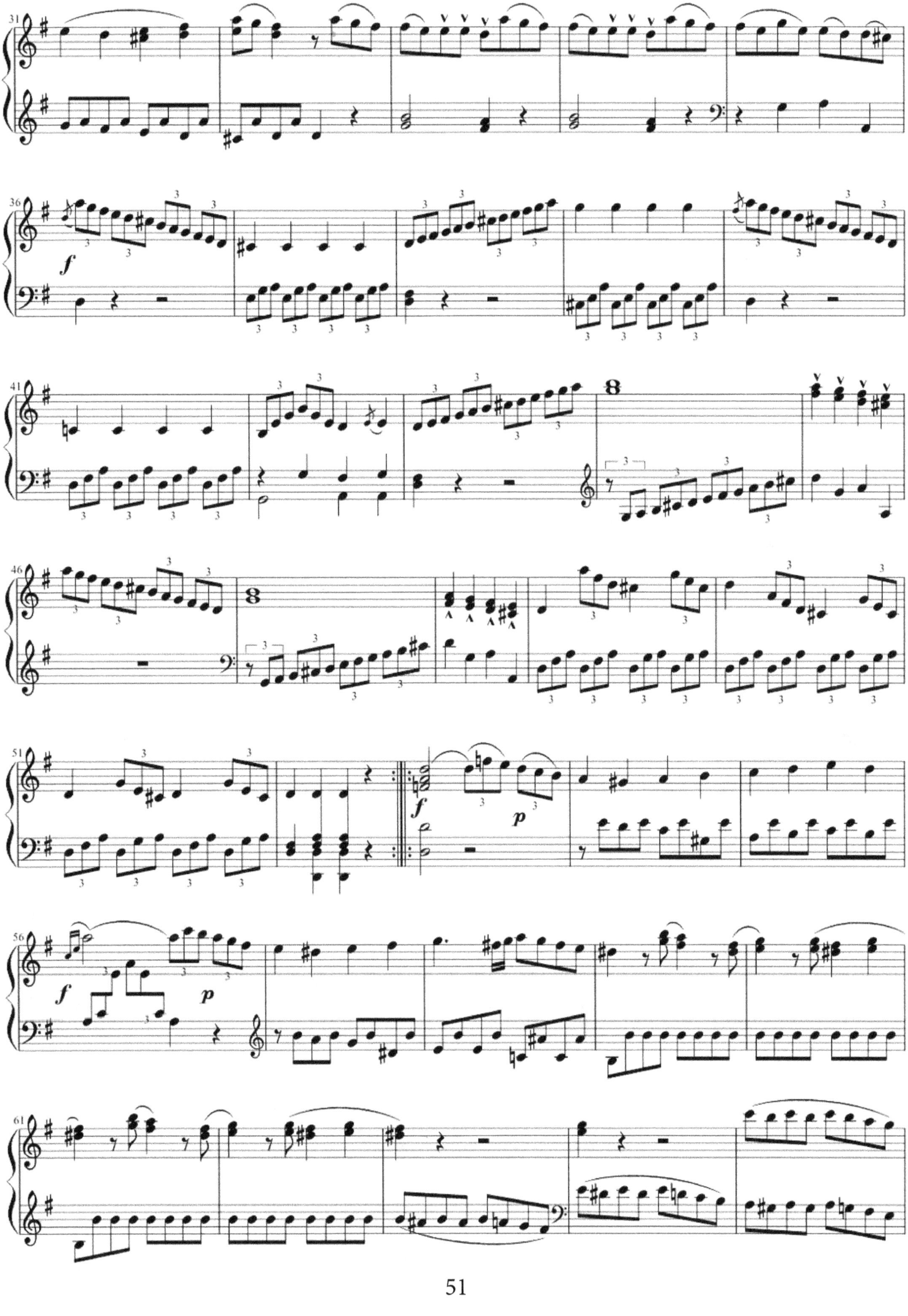
31
36
f
41
46
51
f
p
56
f
p
61

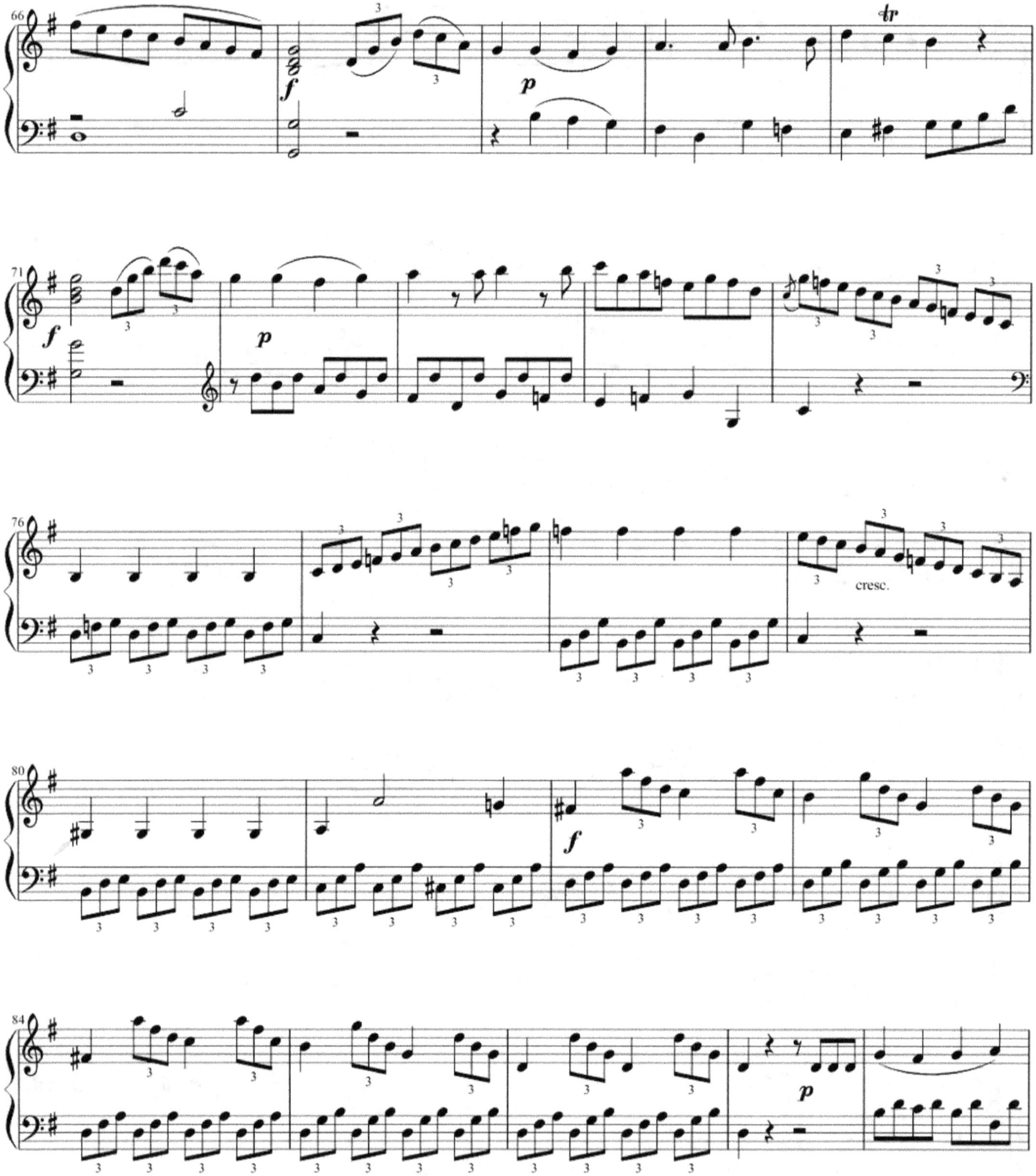
cresc.

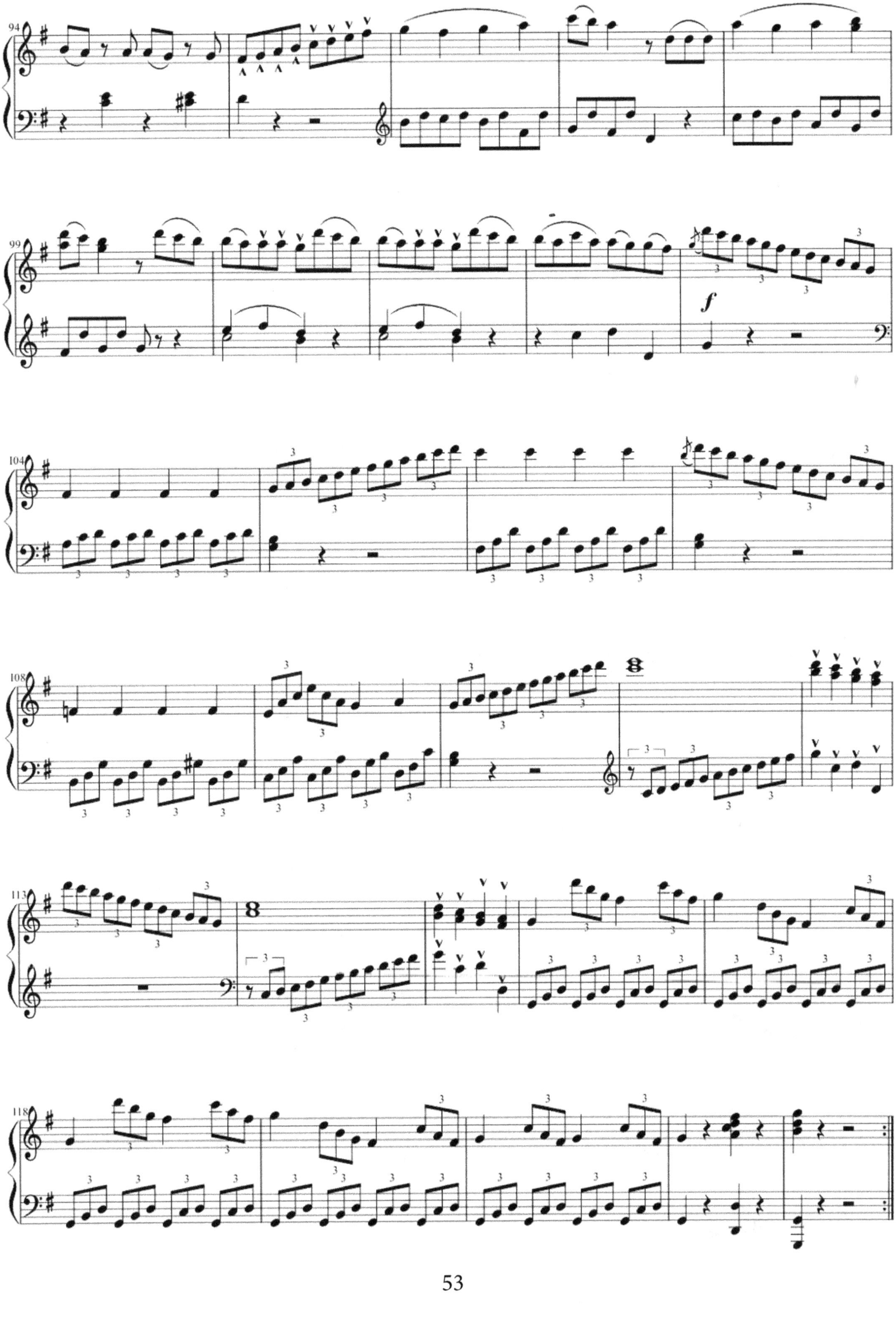
94
99
f
104
108
113
118

Opus 36, No 5

Muzio Clementi

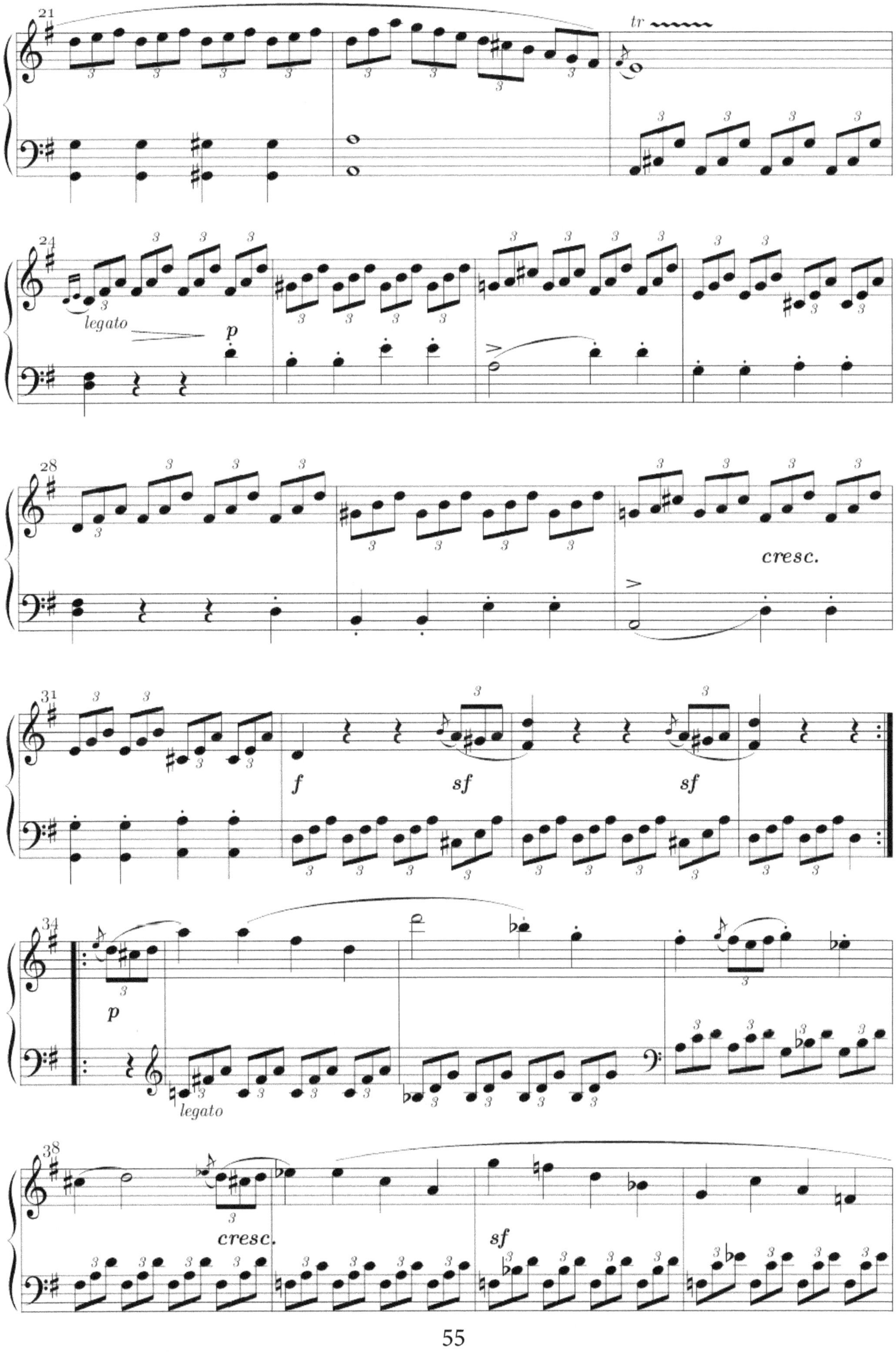
tr
legato
p
cresc.
f
sf
sf
p
legato
cresc.
sf

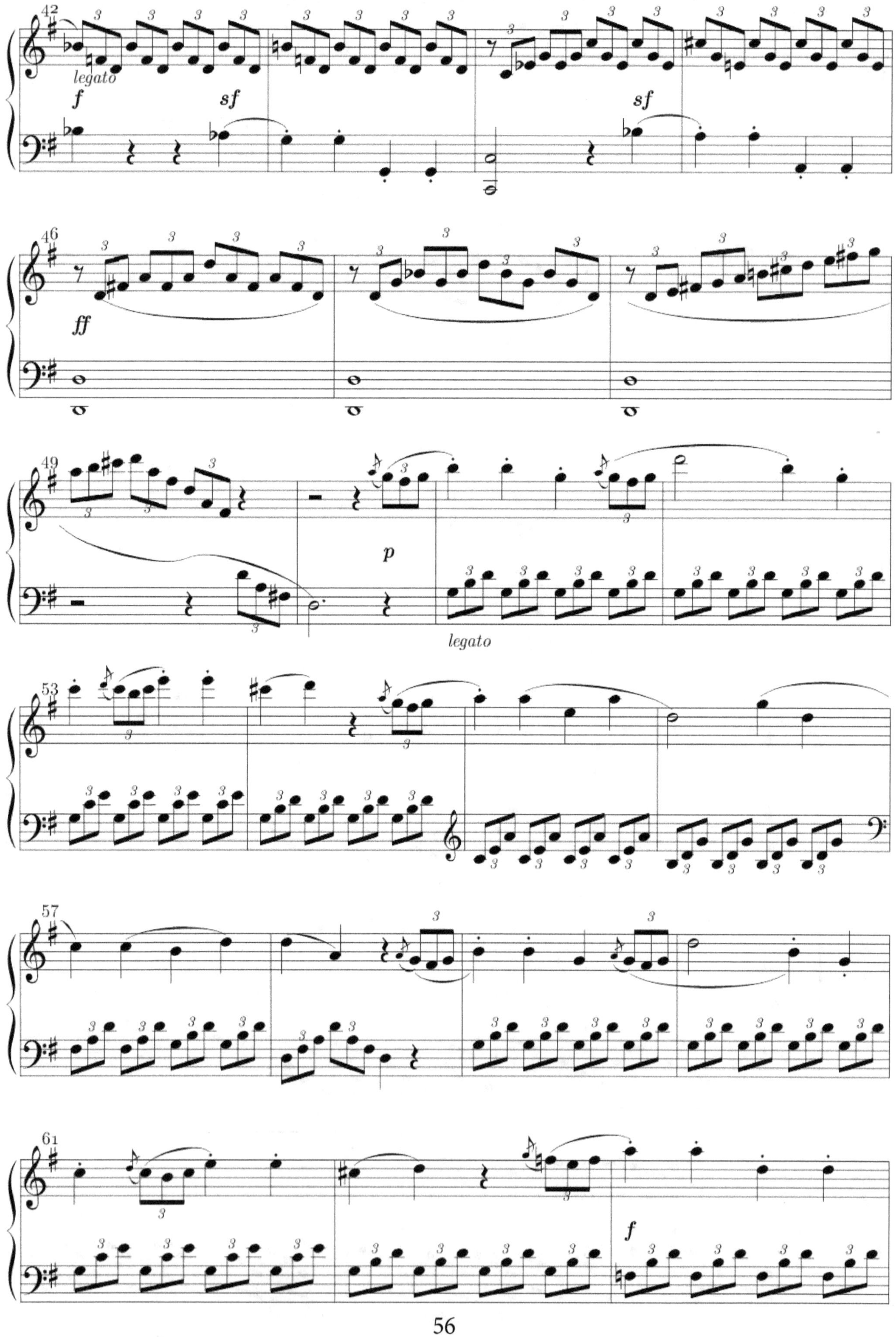
42
legato
f
sf
sf
46
ff
49
p
legato
53
57
61
f

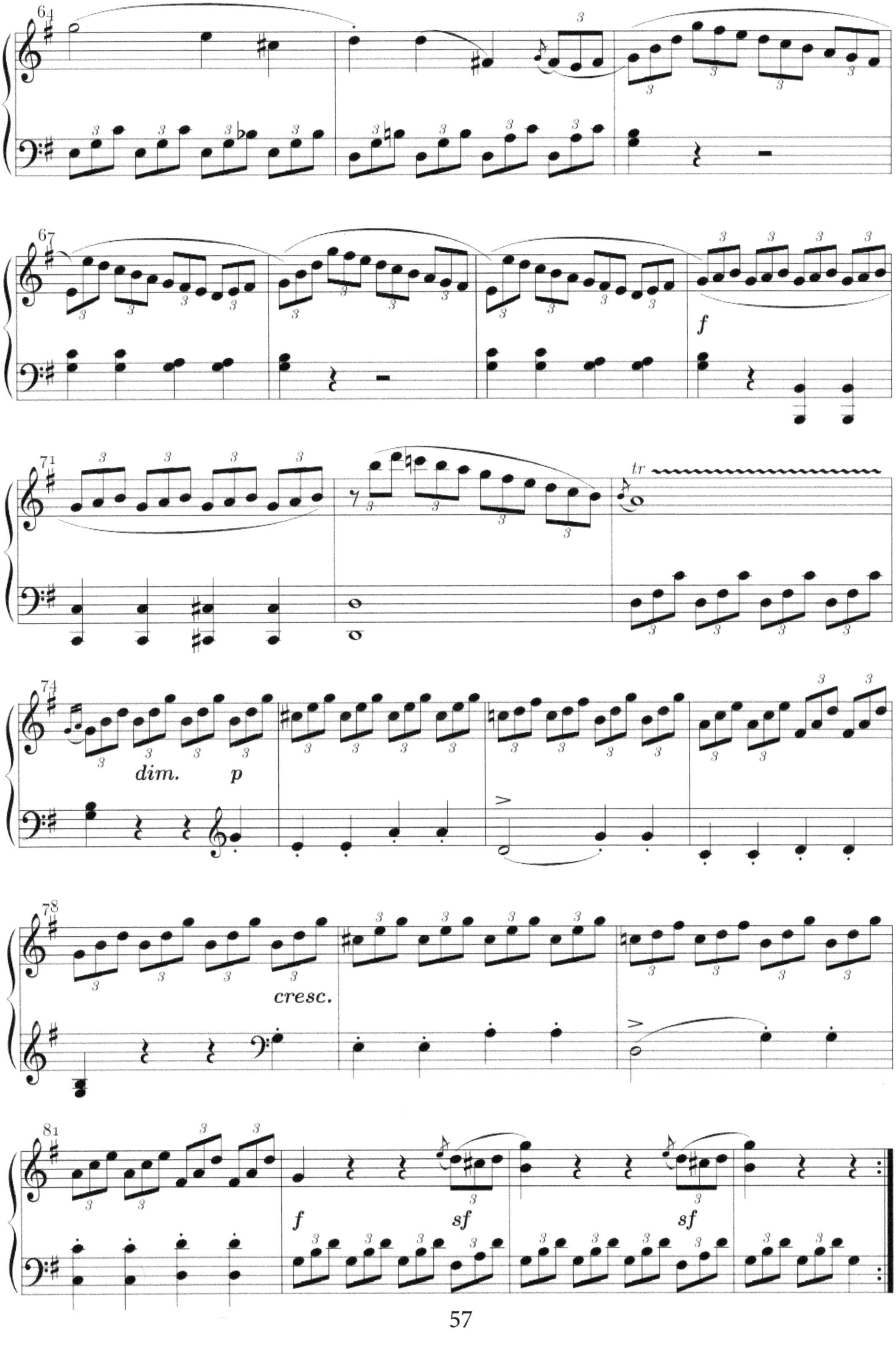
64
67
f
71
tr
74
dim.
p
78
cresc.
81
f
sf
sf

GRADE 6

Nocturne in C# Minor

Opus 27, No 1

Frédéric François Chopin

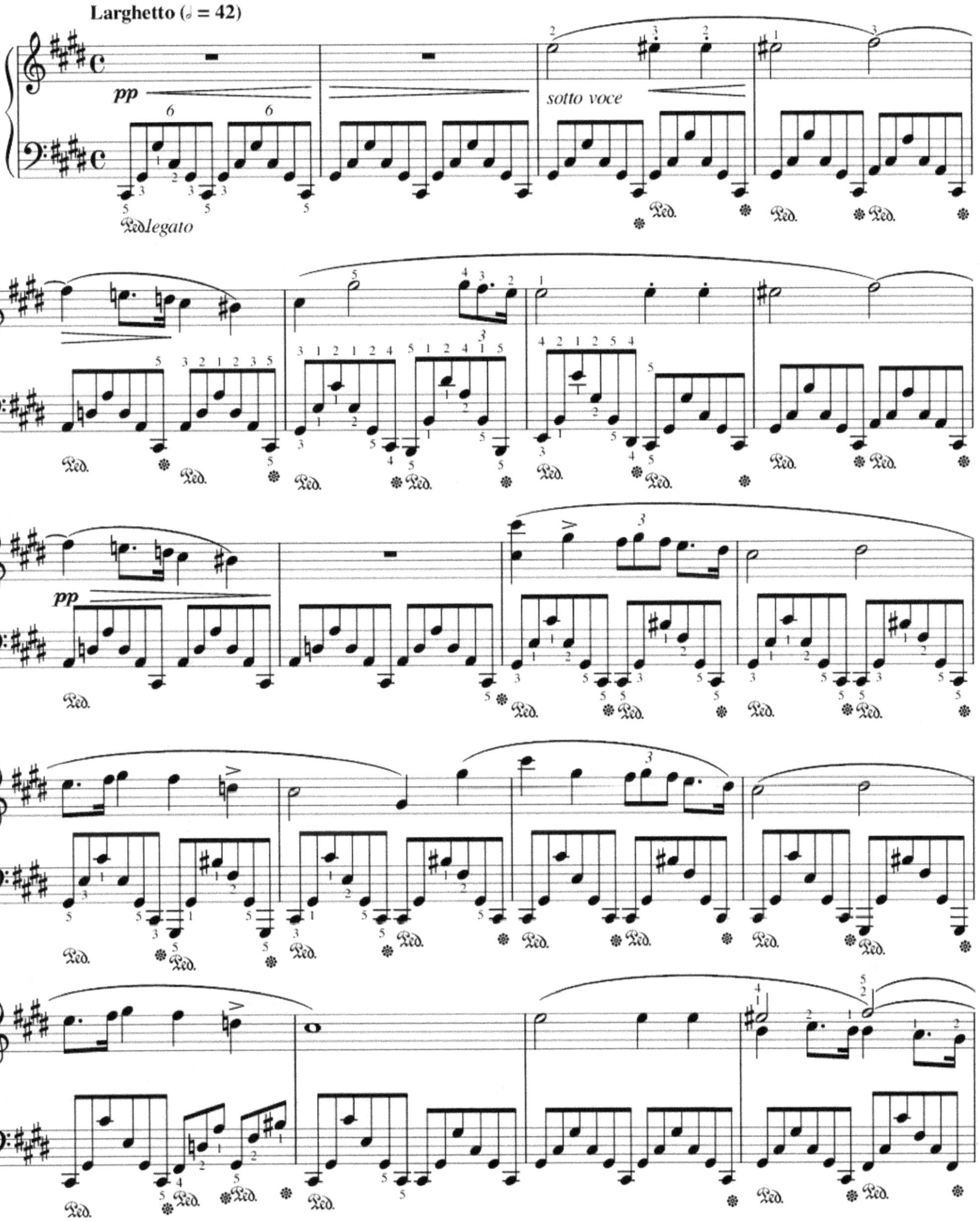

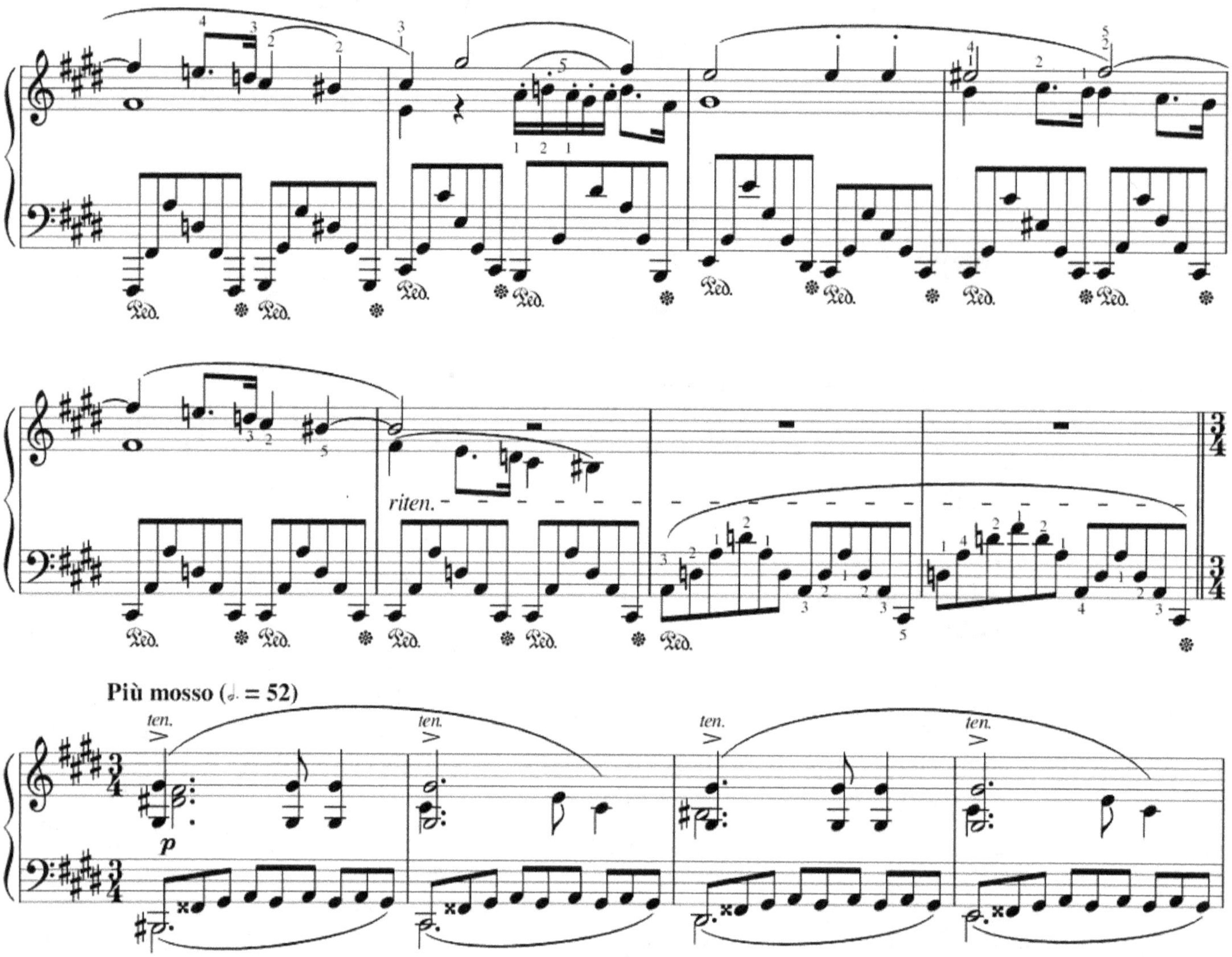
riten.
Più mosso (𝅗𝅥. = 52)
ten.
p
poco a poco cresc.
f
fz
Ped.

sempre più stretto ed
cresc.
fz Ped.
appassionato
ff
sostenuto
fff
riten.
dim.
agitato
sotto voce
poco a poco cresc.
ed accel.

riten.
con anima
ten.
stretto.
f
pp
cresc. ed accel.
fff
con forza
Ped.

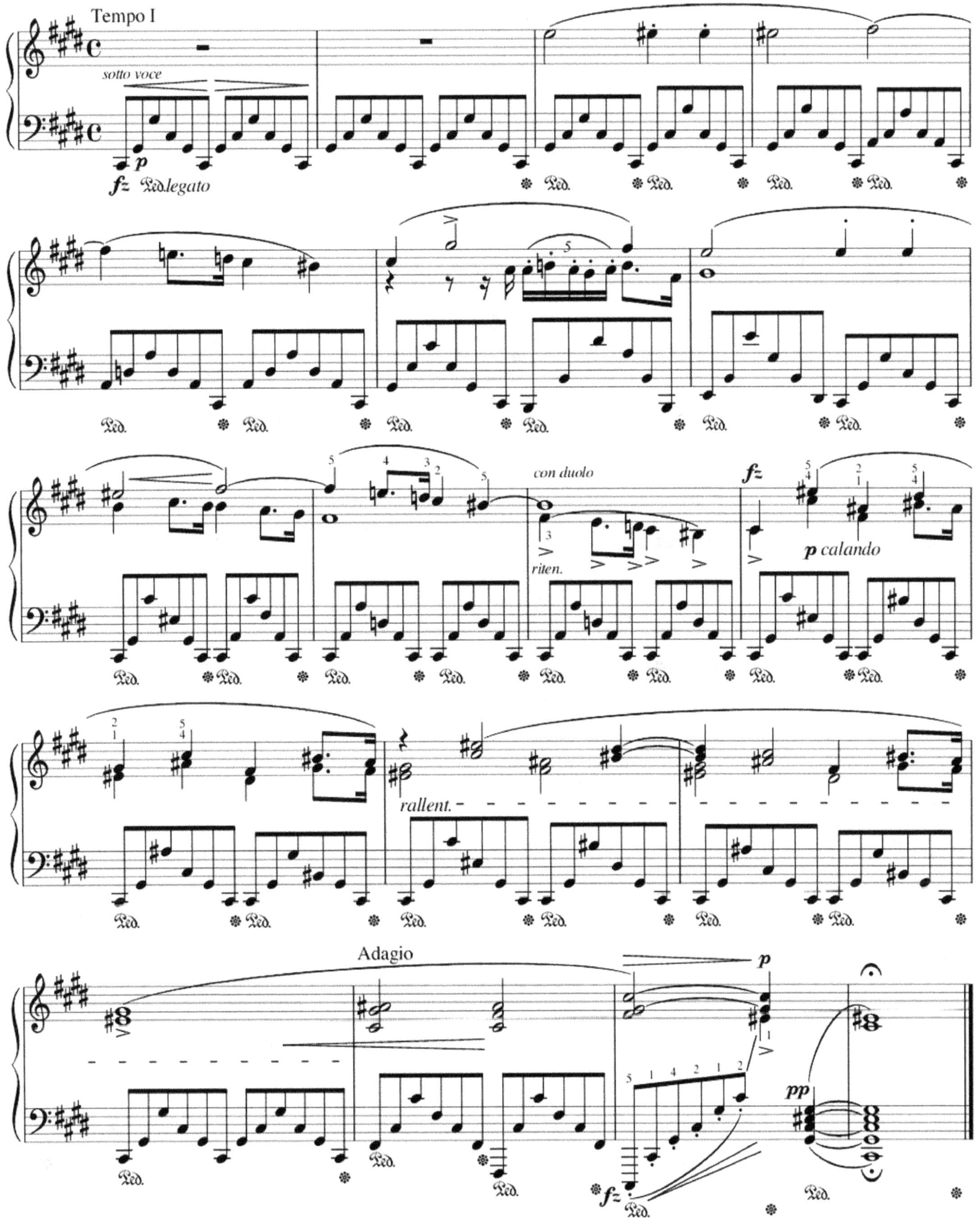
Tempo I
sotto voce
fz
p
legato
con duolo
riten.
fz
p calando
rallent.
Adagio
p
fz
pp

Nocturne in D♭ Major
Opus 27, No 2

Frédéric François Chopin

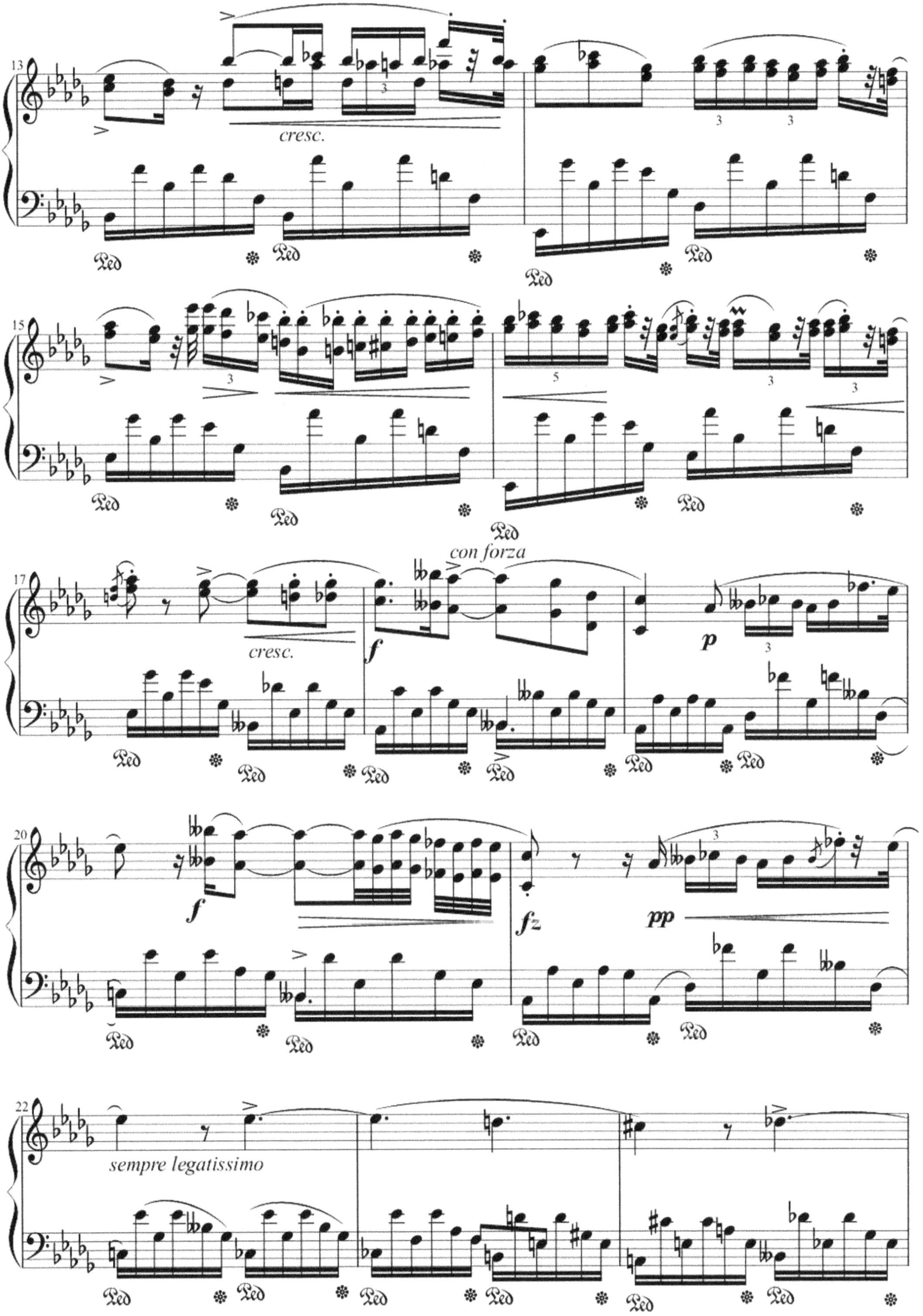
13
cresc.
15
17
cresc.
con forza
f
p
20
f
fz
pp
22
sempre legatissimo

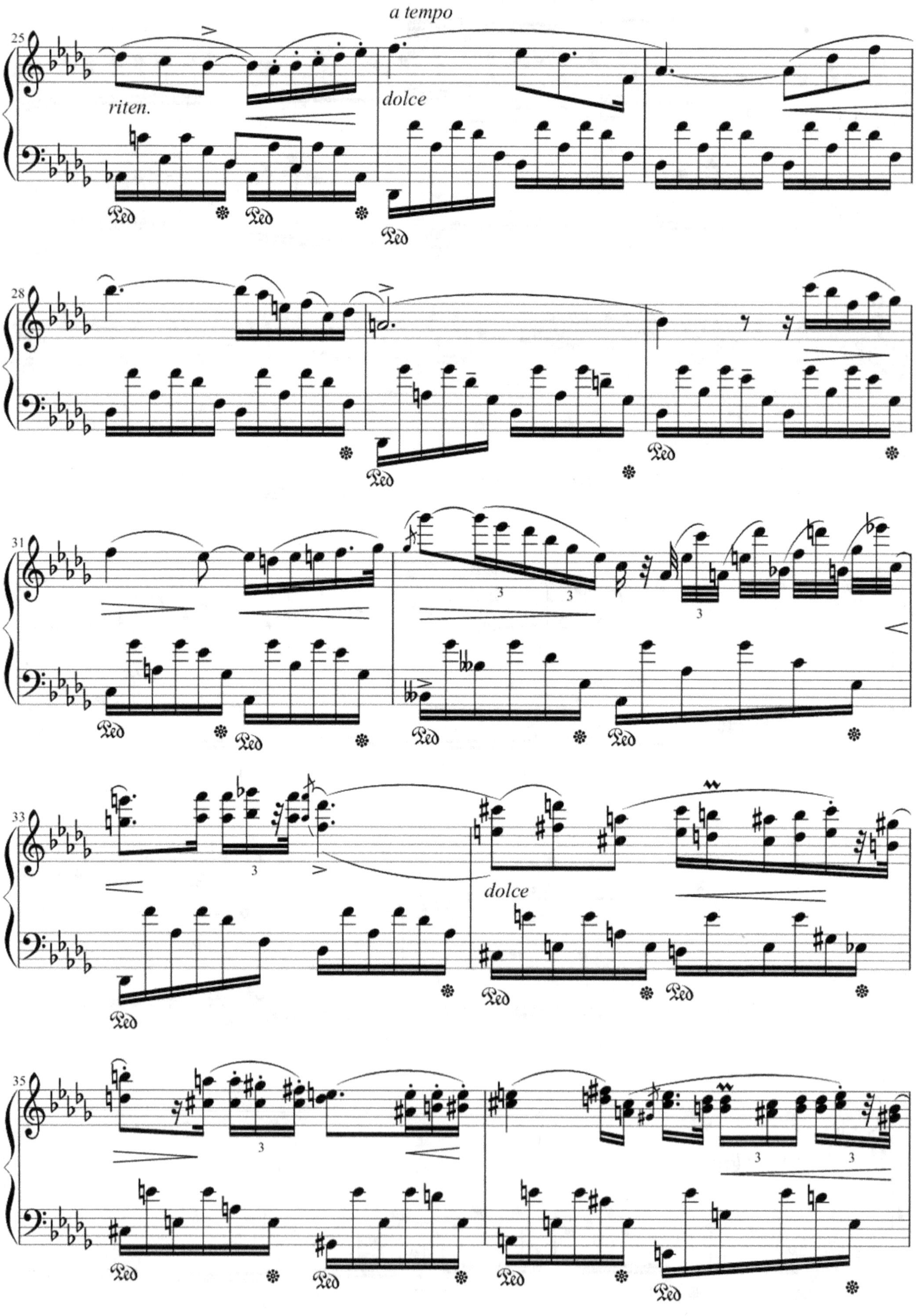
a tempo
25
riten.
dolce
28
31
33
dolce
35

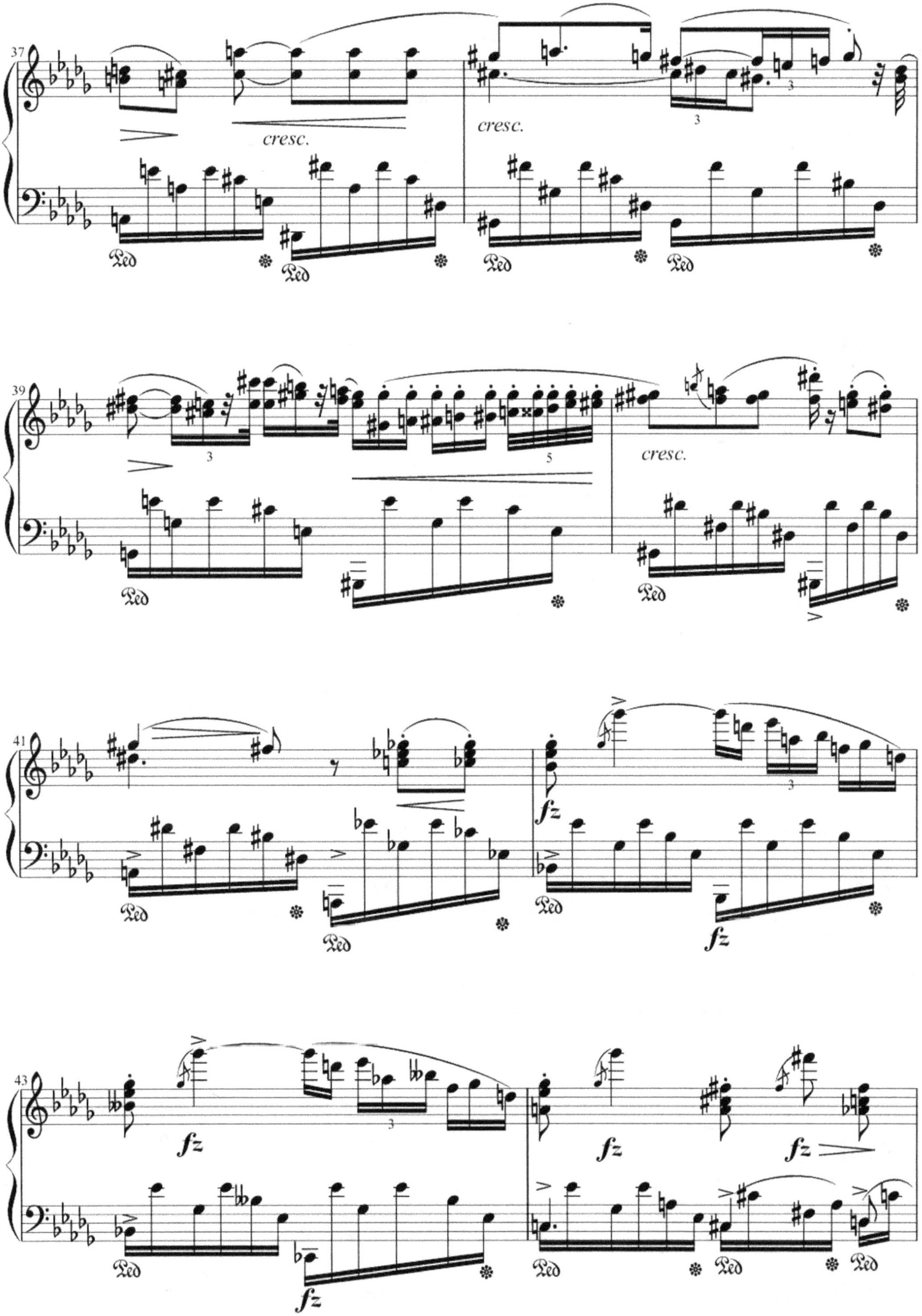
37
cresc.
cresc.
Ped
39
cresc.
41
fz
43
fz

70

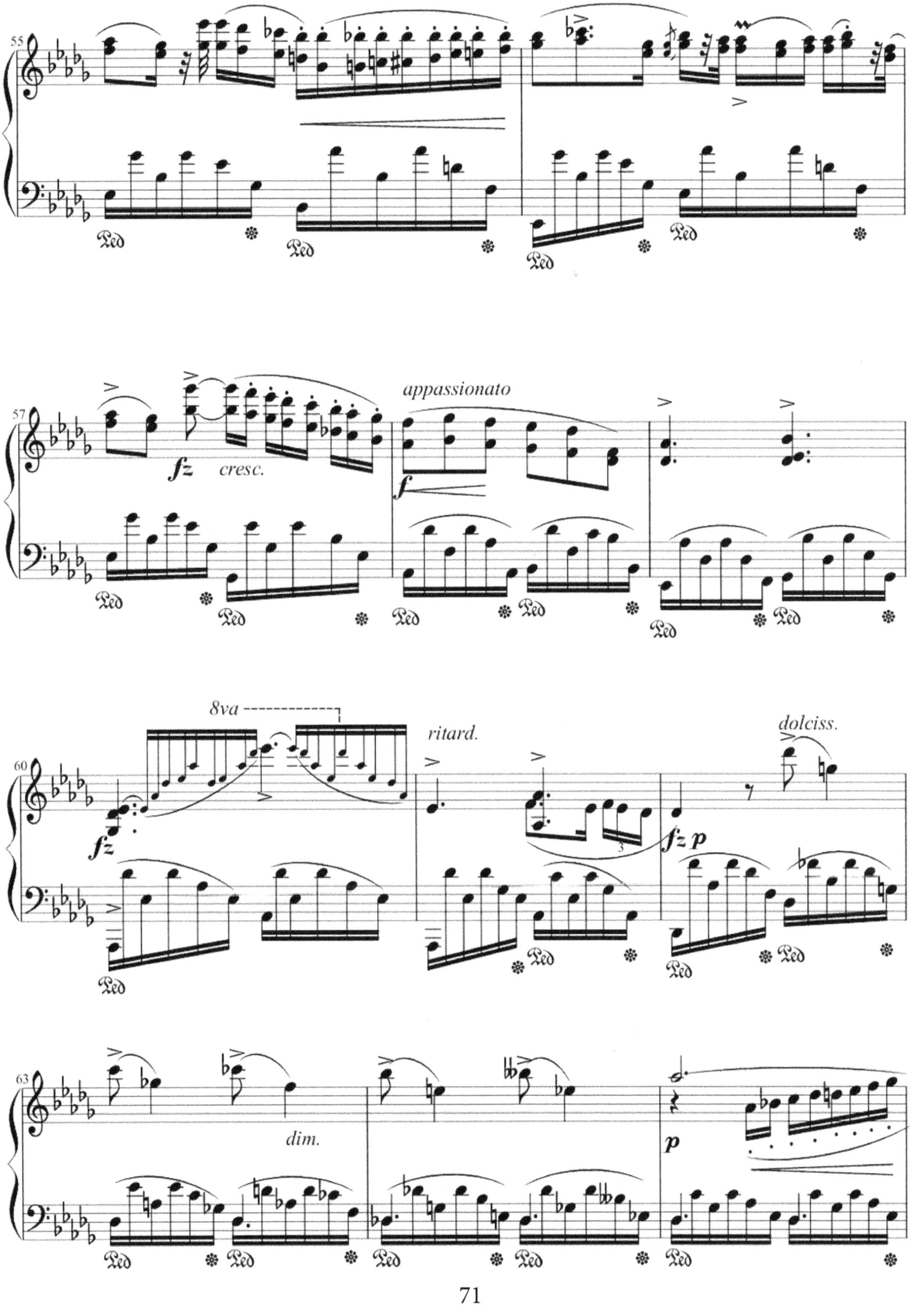
55
57
fz
cresc.
appassionato
f
60
8va
ritard.
dolciss.
fz p
63
dim.
p
Ped

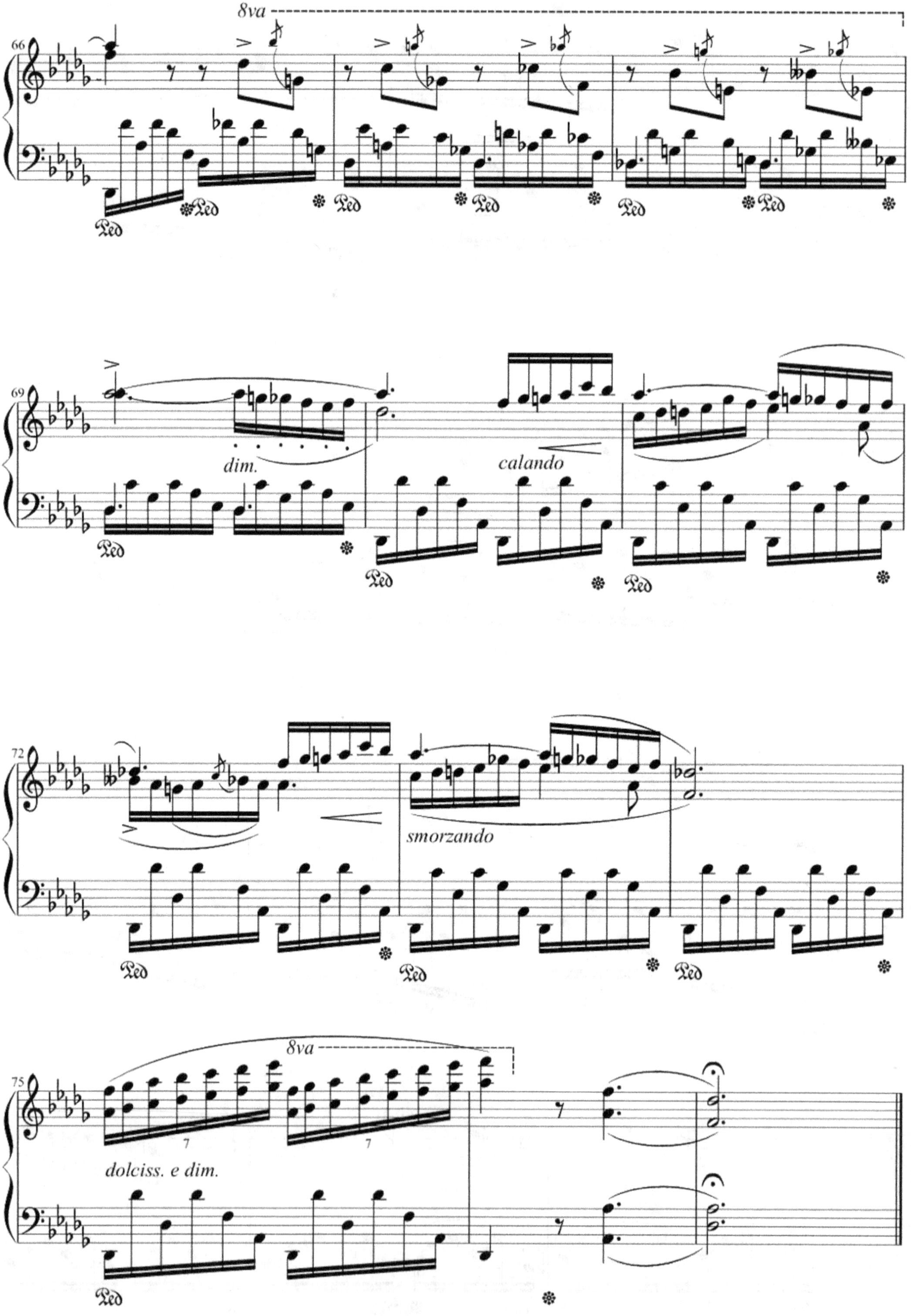
66
8va
69
dim.
calando
72
smorzando
75
8va
7
7
dolciss. e dim.
Ped

Invention in A Minor
BWV 784

Johann Sebastian Bach

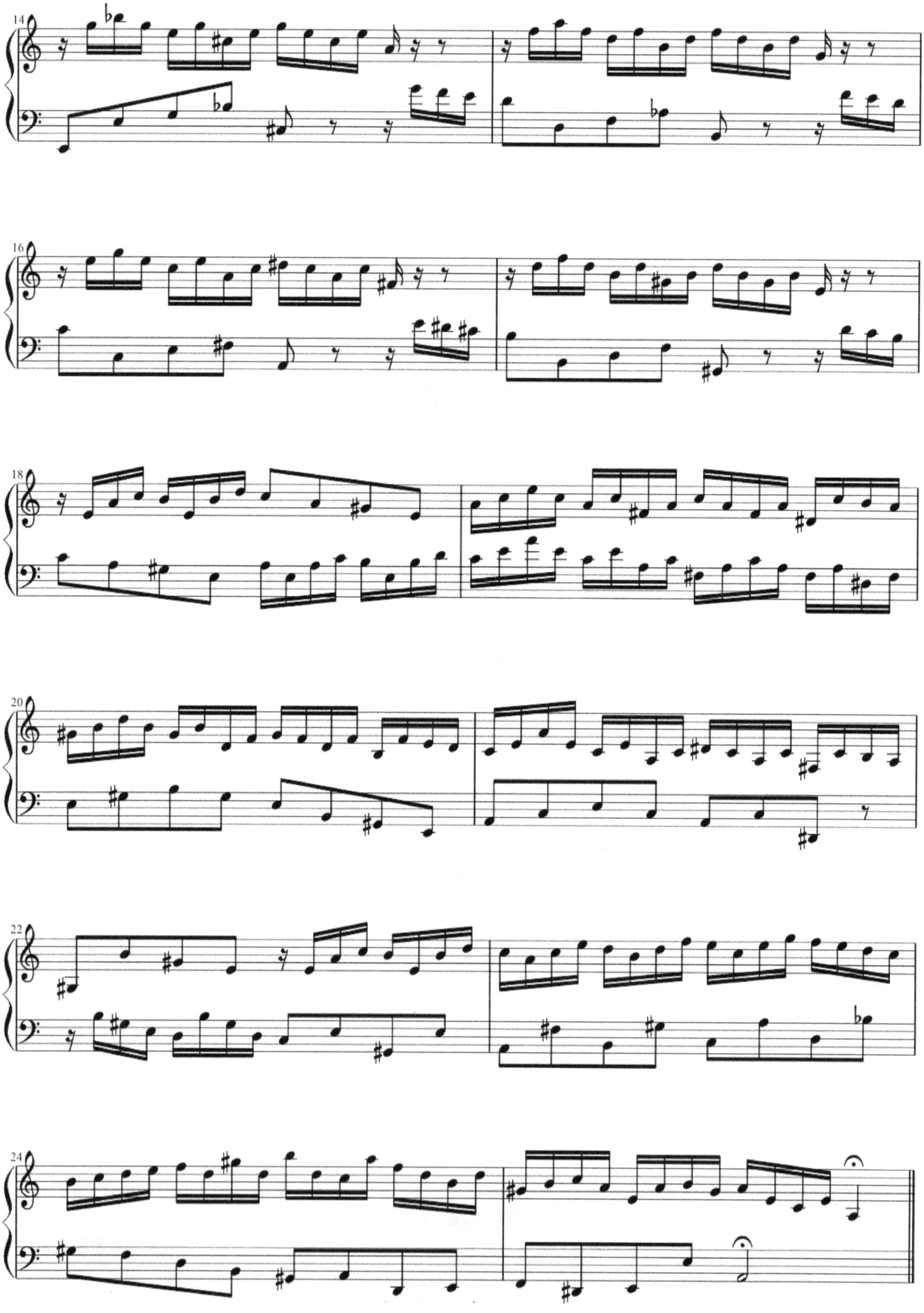

Prelude and Fugue in A Minor

Johann Sebastian Bach

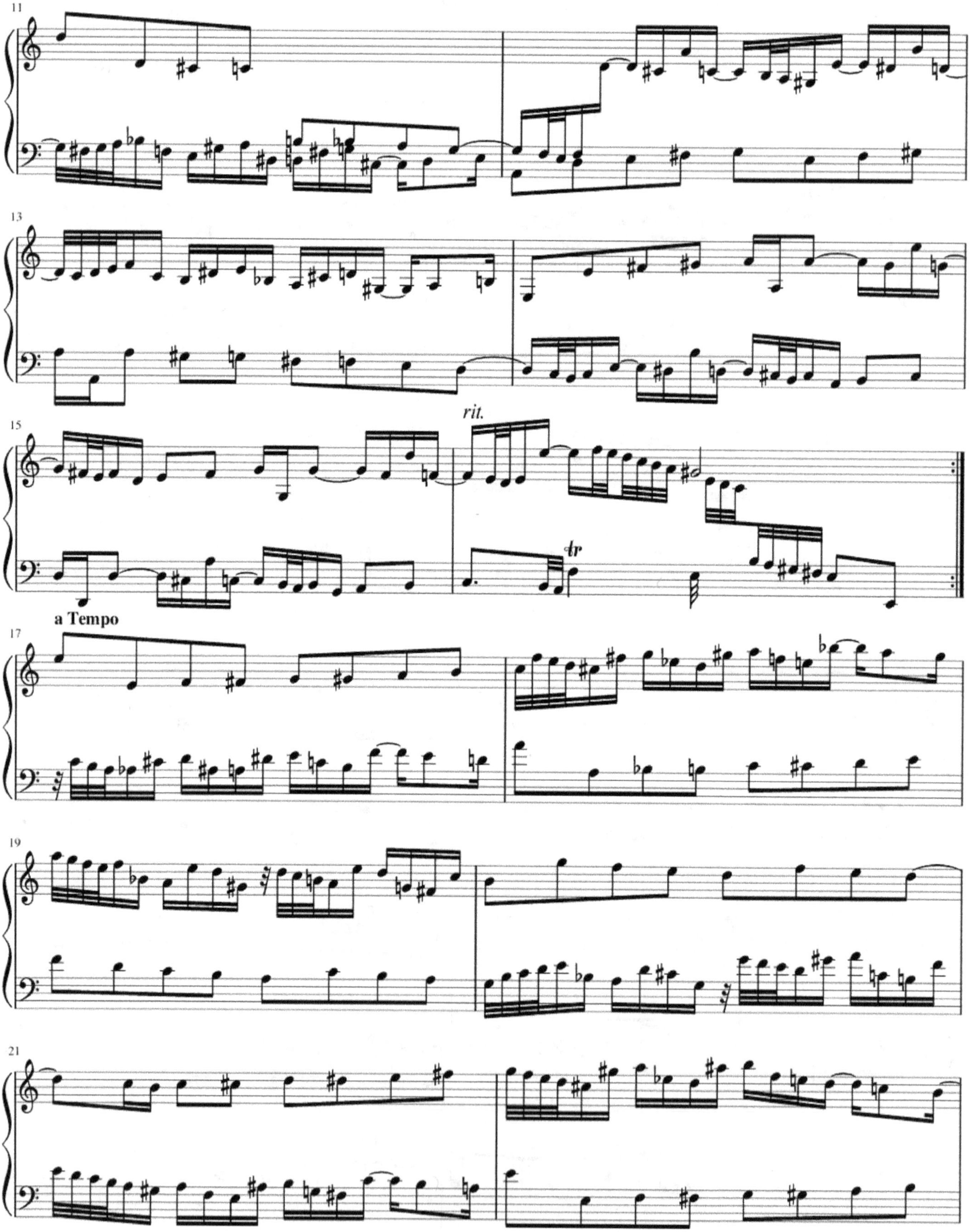
11
13
15
rit.
tr
a Tempo
17
19
21

II. Fugue (♩ = 60)

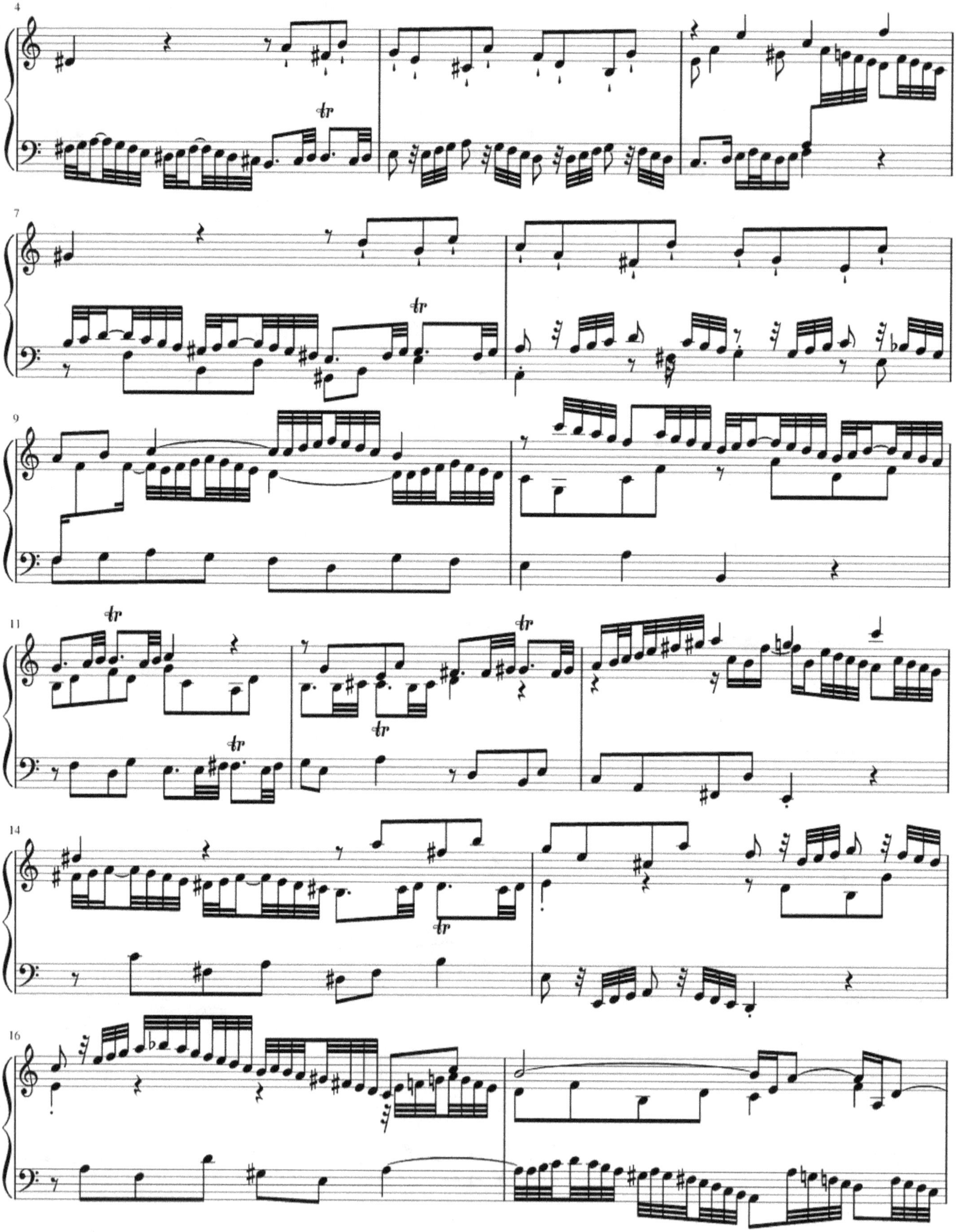
4
tr
7
tr
9
11
tr
tr
tr
tr
14
tr
16

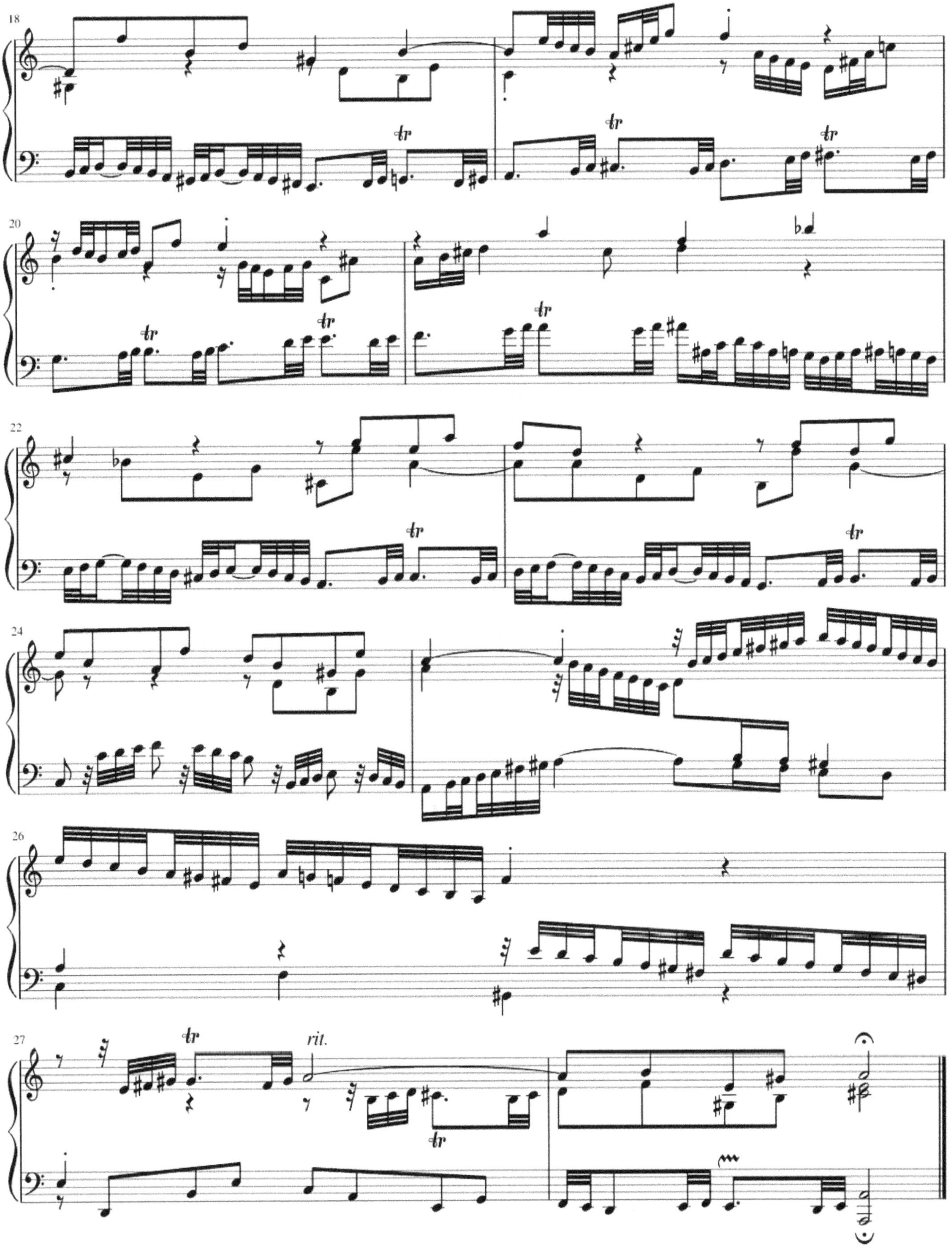
18
tr
20
22
24
26
27
rit.

Sinfonia No 11 in G minor
BWV 797

Johann Sebastian Bach

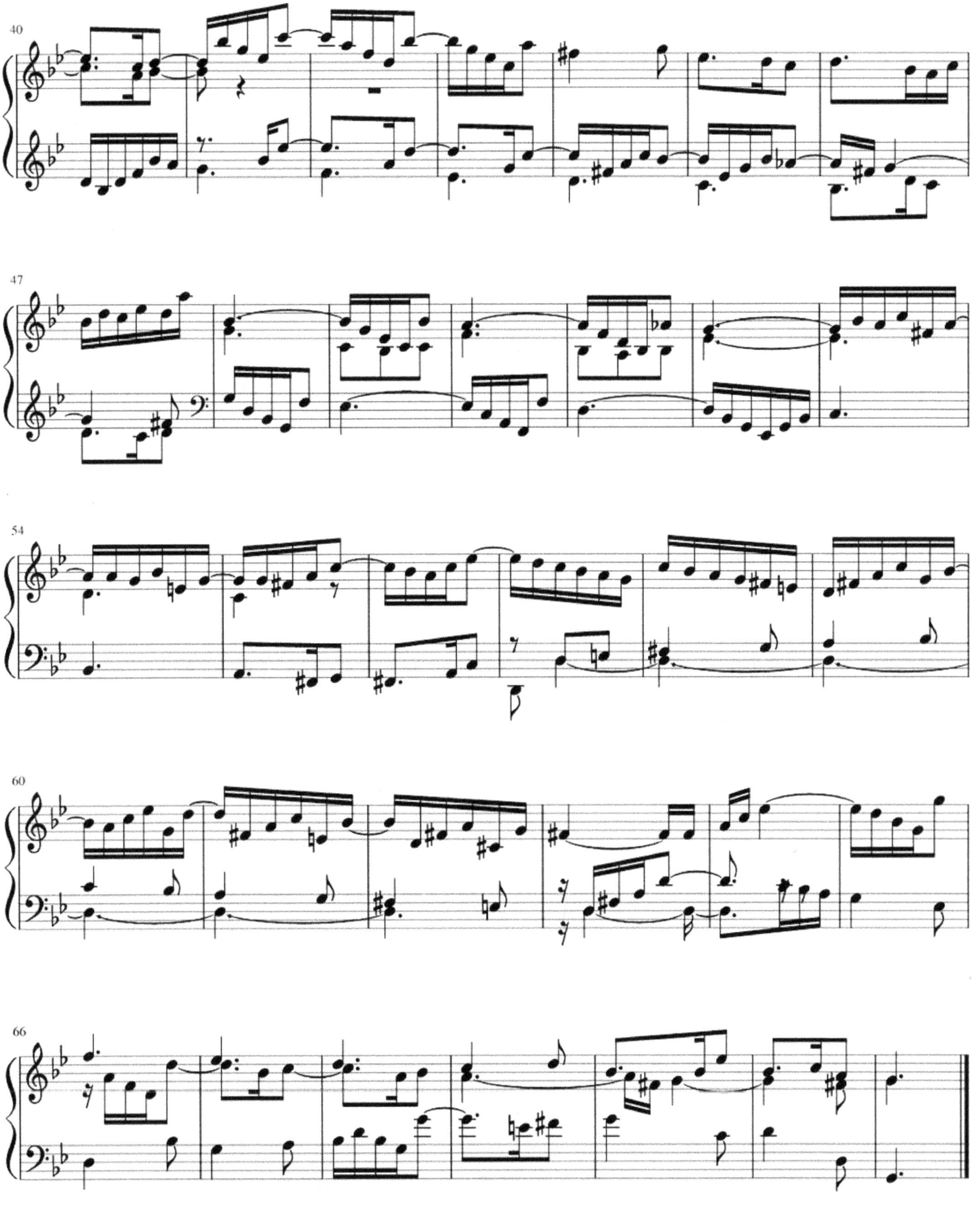
40
47
54
60
66

Sonata No 1 in F Minor
1 Allegro

Ludwig Van Beethoven

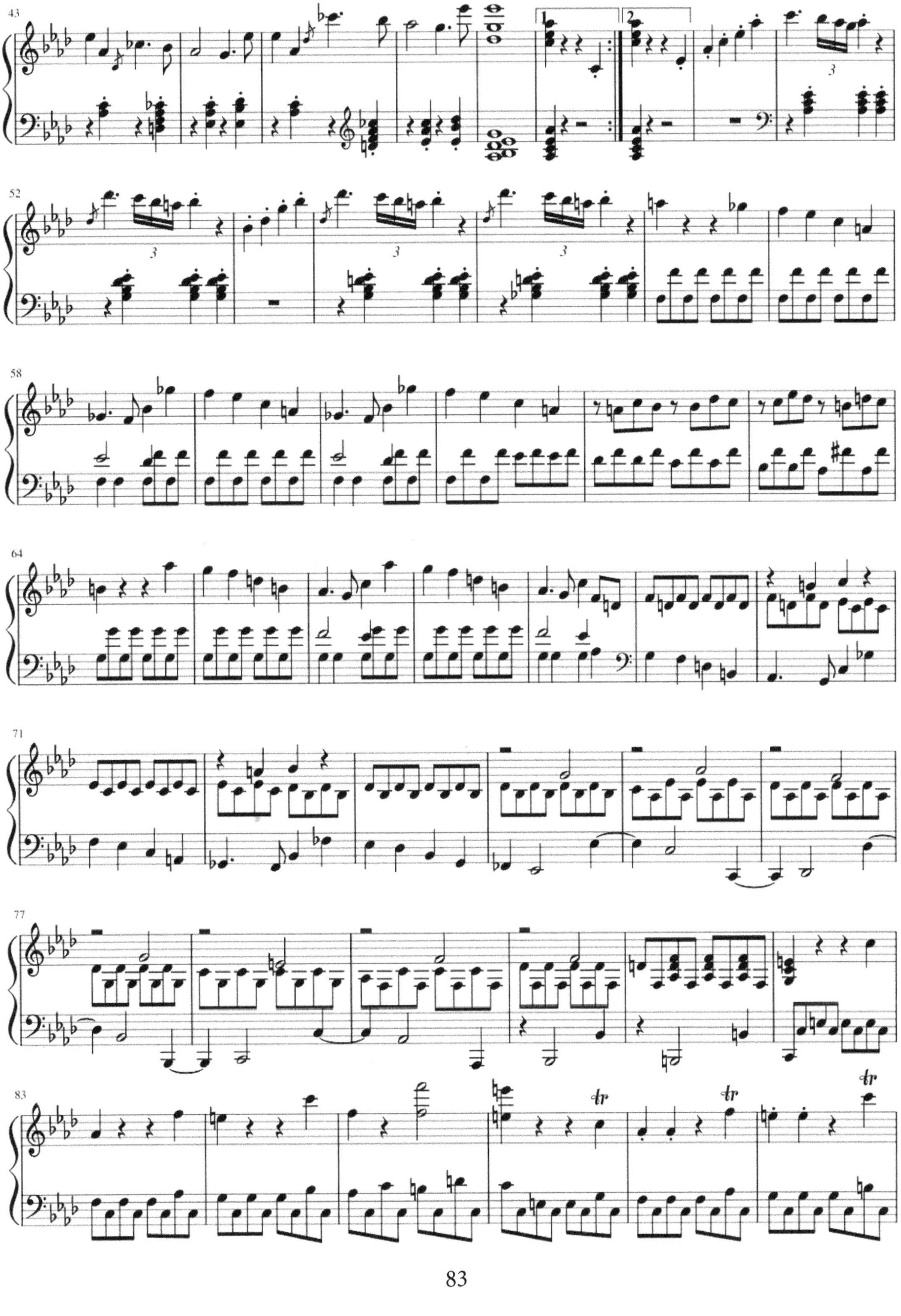
43
1.
2.
52
58
64
71
77
83
tr

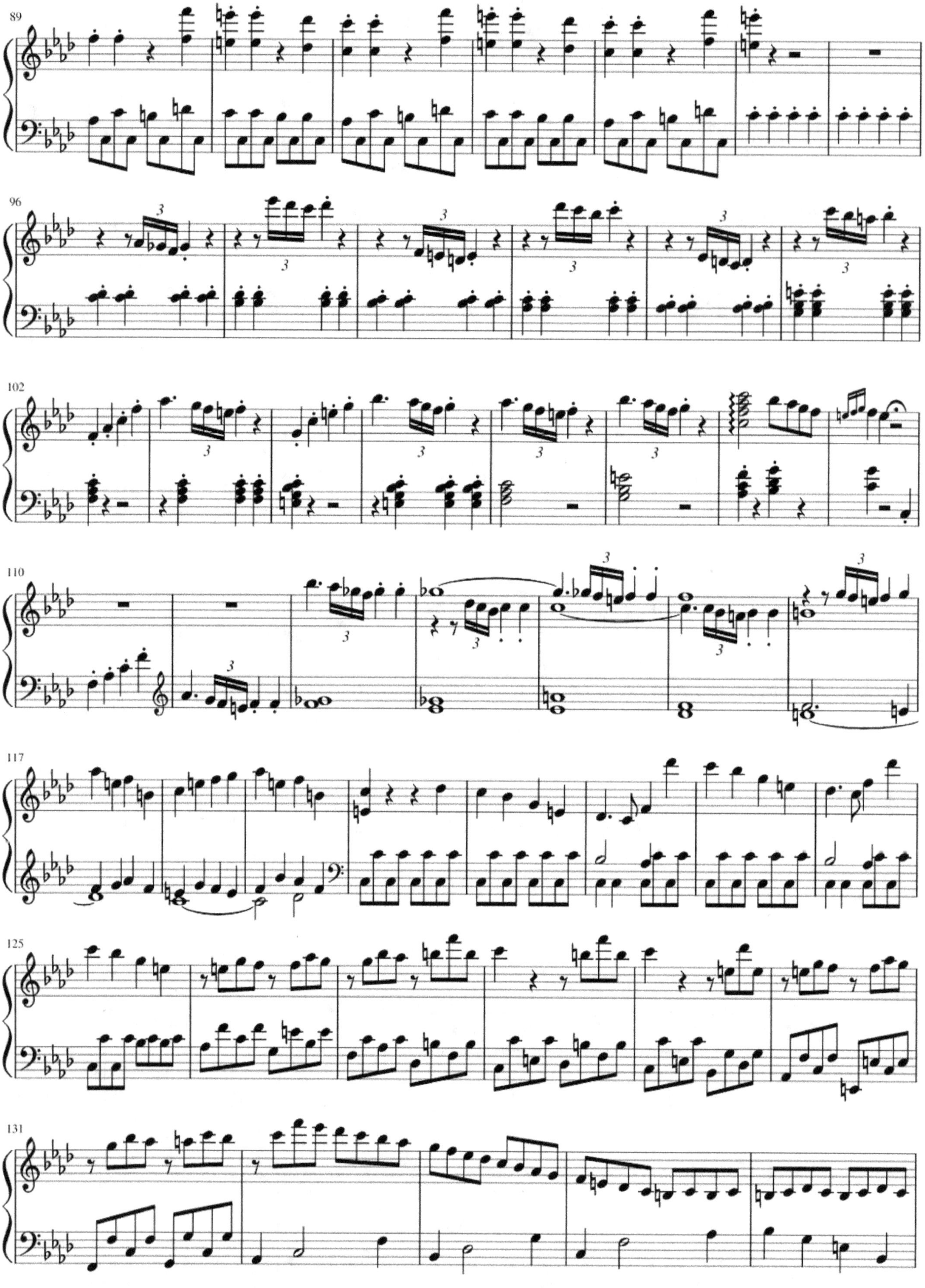
89
96
102
110
117
125
131

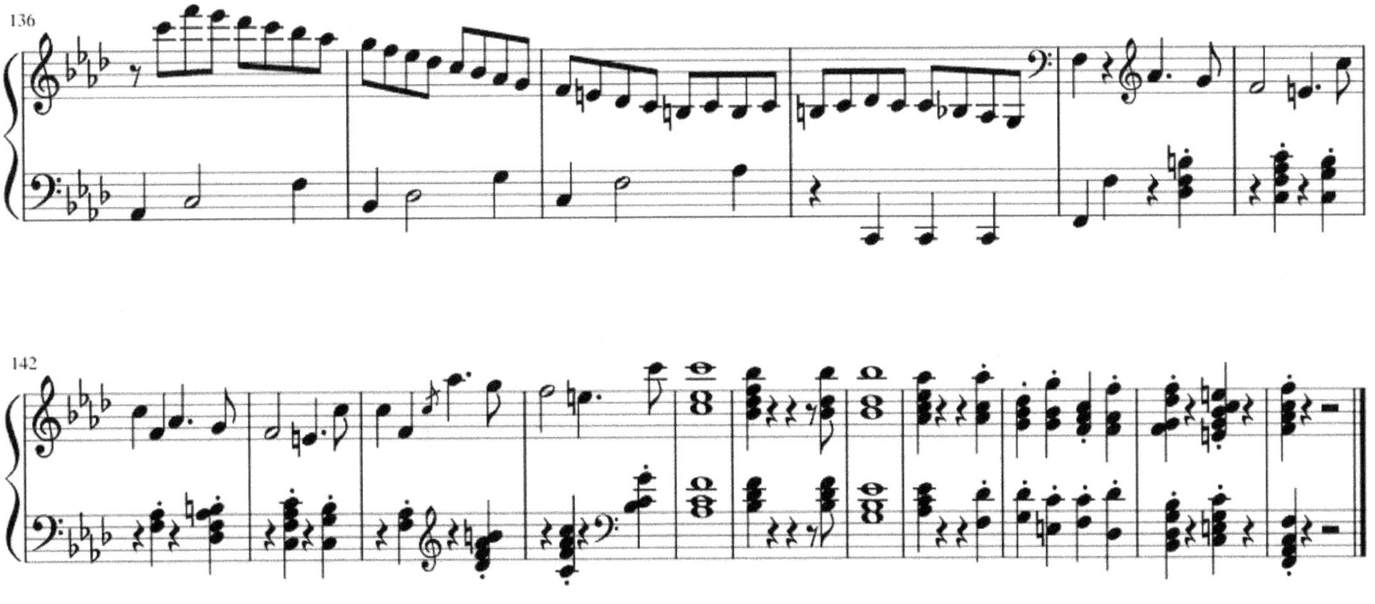
136
142

Rondo, Sonata No 16 in C
3rd Movement, K.545

Wolfgang Amadeus Mozart

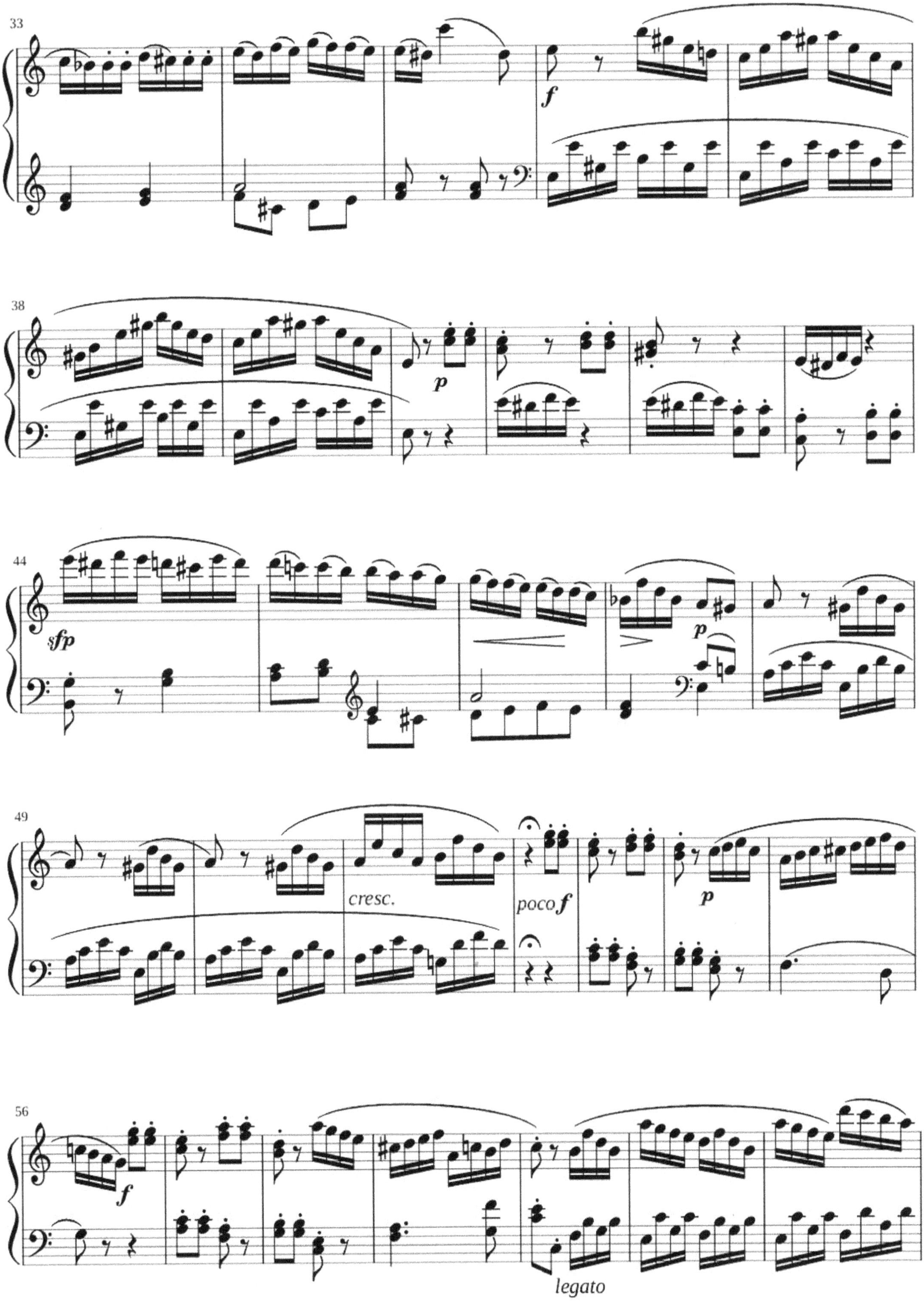
33
38
44
49
cresc.
poco f
56
legato

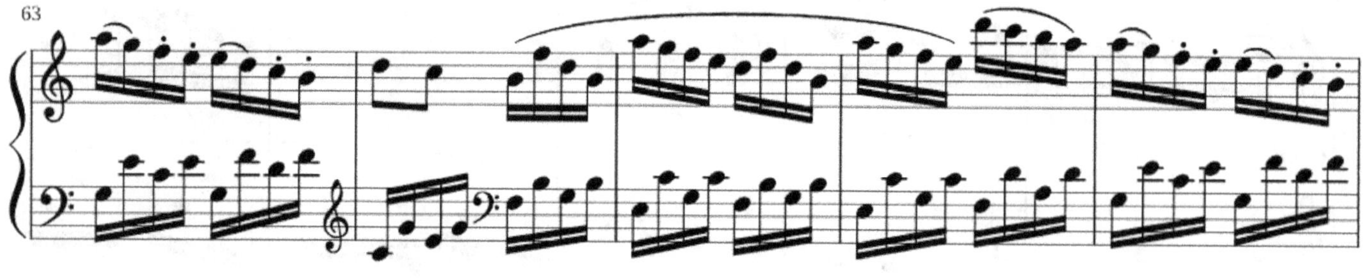
63

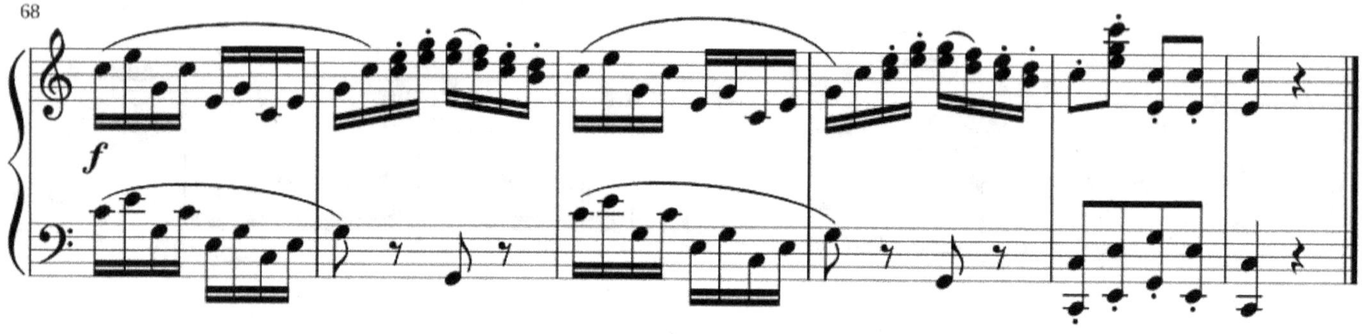
68
f

Sonata K.283
II Adante

Wolfgang Amadeus Mozart

Andante

89

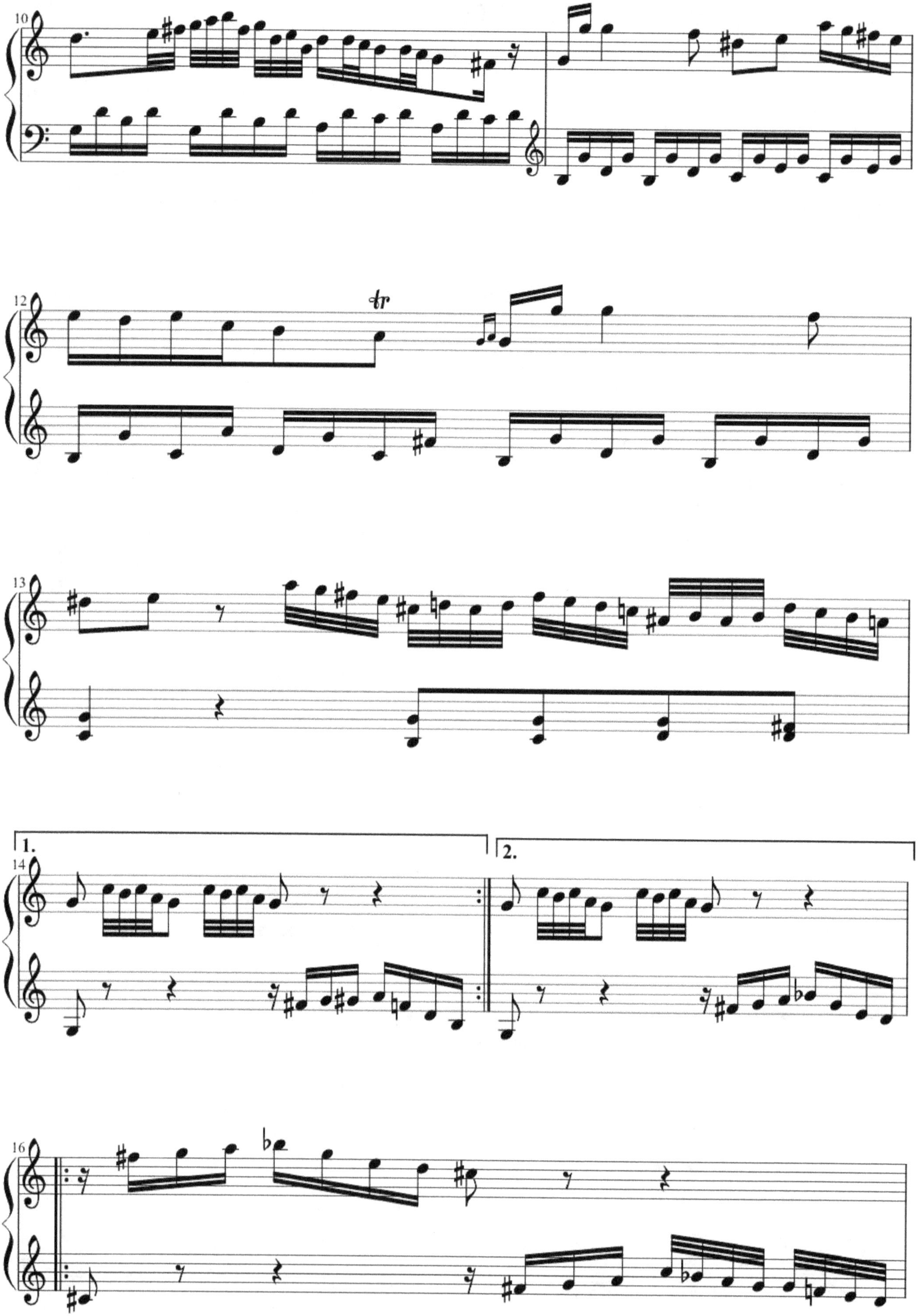
10
12
tr
13
1.
14
2.
16

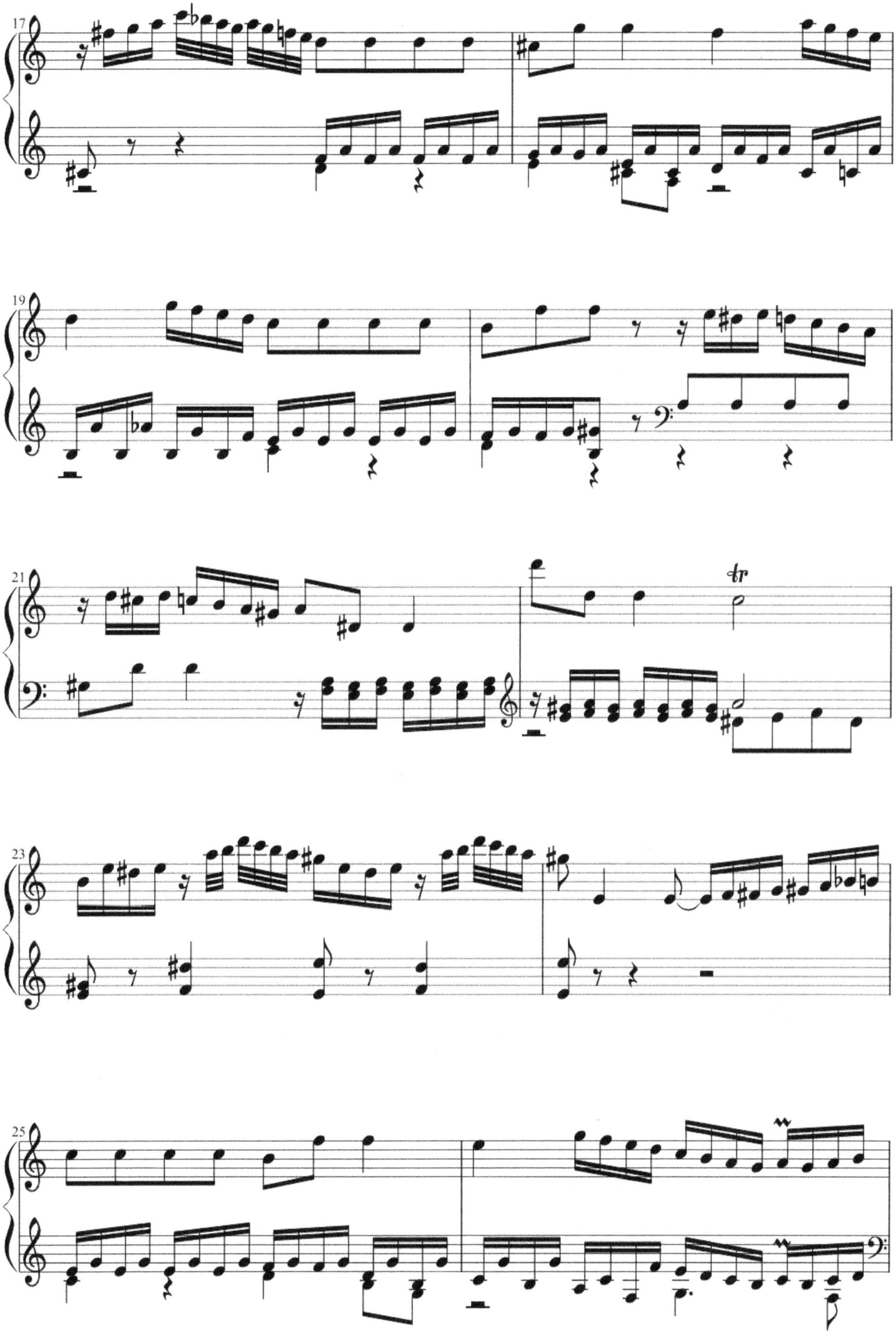
17
19
21
tr
23
25

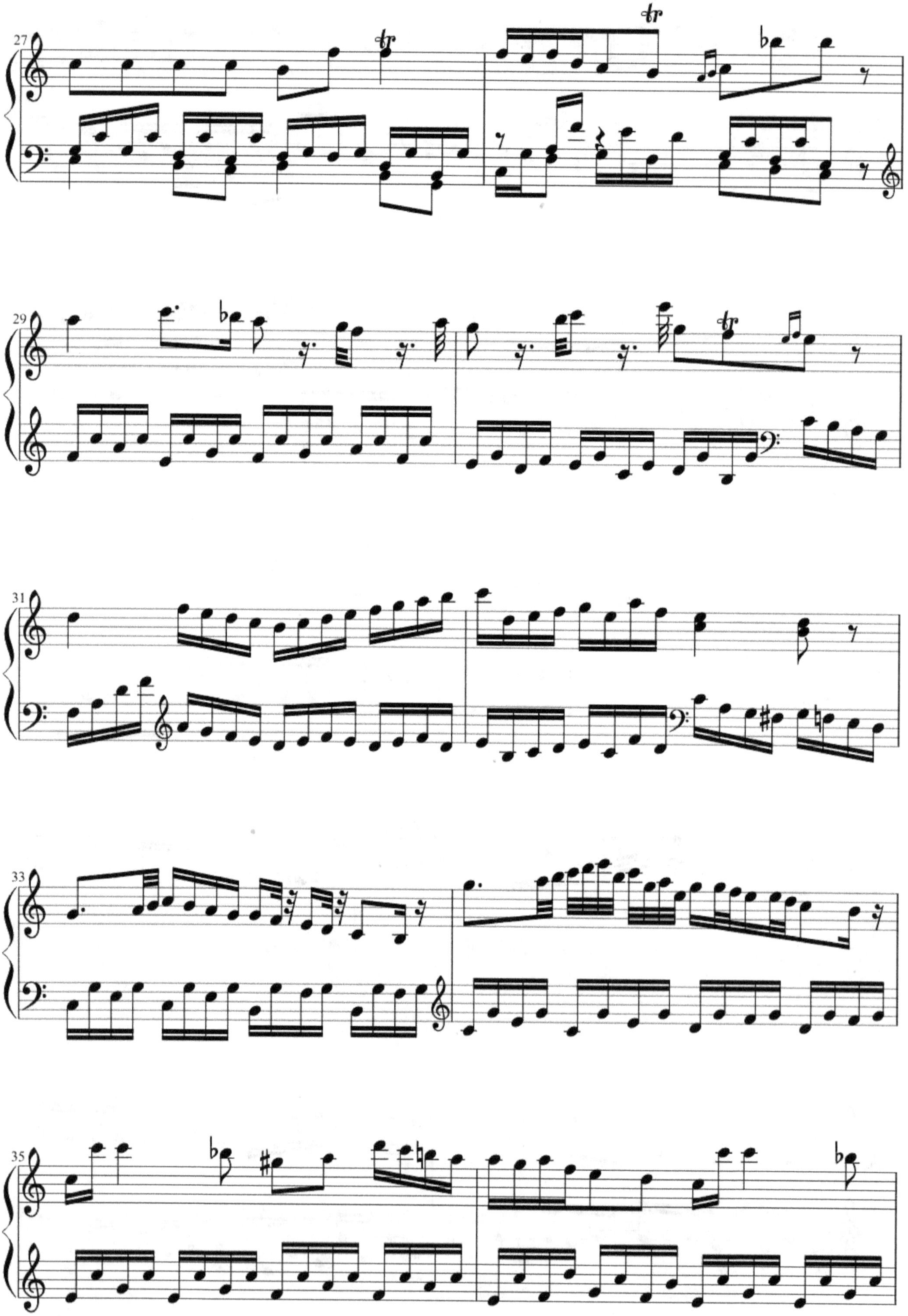
27
tr
tr
29
tr
31
33
35

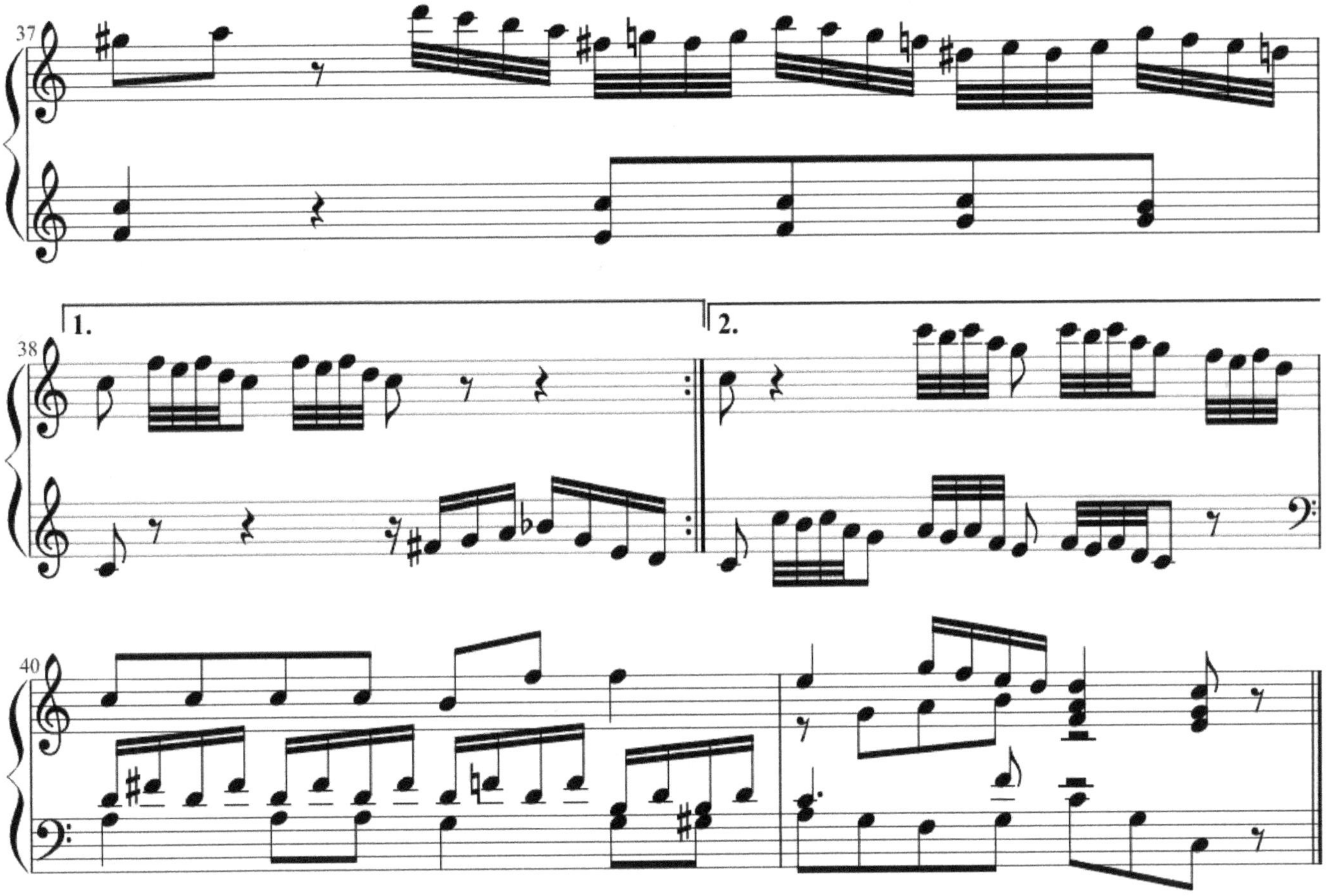
37
38
1.
2.
40